Praise

Entering the Secret World of Nature

"Michael Roads adds to his written legacy of open-hearted communication with all of Nature. He transmits his deep experience of communion along with insights about the soul's journey through lifetimes. You'll find how to consciously listen, see, and experience the silence behind all forms, and the greater reality beyond our limited beliefs and illusions, with the skills to be mastered to live in balance with the continuity of life. A treasure."
—*Penelope Smith,* **Founding Animal Communication Specialist, author of *Animal Talk, When Animals Speak, and Animals in Spirit***

* * *

"As long as we perceive Nature as something outside and separate from us, we will learn to encounter it, but never really experience it. As long as we are superficially intent on dissecting the world through our physical senses, we will learn to admire Nature, but never open our hearts to its intrinsic beauty.

We are inseparable from an enormous web of life that pulses through infinite dimensions of reality. How do we remove our blindfolds, learn to listen, eradicate the fears that keep us separate, and relate to this vast impulse of life? How do we become Nature, entering into relationship with a living planet, Gaia, communicating with Her as part of our own being? In his earlier books, Michael writes about his encounters with the great god of Nature, Pan. In this enchanting book, he goes even further, not only coming to recognize Pan as the deepest essence of his own being, but sharing with us how we can each do so too!

— *Kiara Windrider,* **author of** *Gaia Luminous: Emergence of the New Earth*

* * *

This book is a masterpiece of inspired and inspiring writing, with many revelatory sections. It reflects a lifetime devoted to the subject.
— *Brian Longhurst,* **author of The Kingdom Series**

* * *

"In his inimitable way the brilliant metaphysicist Michael Roads conveys yet again the immeasurable power that lies in being able to really perceive Truth. This time supplemented by the most comprehensible instructions on how to enter the secret world of nature. A must read for everyone who wishes to overcome the limitations of his or her own mind . . . and the influence of others!"

— *Elisabeth Karsten,* author of the novel, *YS*

Entering
The
SECRET
WORLD
of
NATURE

Award-winning and best-selling author of

Talking with Nature *and* **Journey Into Nature**

MICHAEL J. ROADS

Entering
—— *The* ——
SECRET
WORLD
—— *of* ——
NATURE

SIX DEGREES PUBLISHING GROUP
PORTLAND · OREGON

ENTERING THE SECRET WORLD OF NATURE

For information contact Six Degrees Publishing Group by email:
publisher@sixdegreespublishing.com

FIRST ENGLISH LANGUAGE EDITION

ISBN: 978-1-942497-39-4
EBook ISBN: 978-1-942497-40-0

Six Degrees Publishing Group
5331 S. W. Macadam Avenue, Suite 258
Portland, OR 97239
SixDegreesPublishing.com

"Books that transcend the ordinary."

Published in the USA
Printed simultaneously in the USA, United Kingdom and Australia

1 3 7 9 10 8 6 4 2

DEDICATION

This book is dedicated to my beautiful, beloved wife, Carolyn.
I have seen enough of human life in my many decades to know that the relationship she and I enjoy is far from common; it is rare. Just as the sun and the moon have evolved into a perfect and balanced relationship for life on Earth, so, without the evolution of ages, she and I orbit each other in perfect harmony and balance. Carolyn is Love, joy and laughter incarnate in my life; a precious blessing that life has bestowed upon me.

Carolyn and Tracey, my daughter, have a large finch aviary to which they are both very dedicated. Carolyn is truly besotted with her finches, spending an hour or two in the aviary every day. She has developed a real affinity with these tiny colourful birds, her "flying jewels" as she calls them.

After her hours of quiet observation and contemplation, she often tells me stories about the finches that seem very far-fetched, yet when I spend time with them, I see confirmation.

For example, the male of a pair of painted finches — they all need to be in pairs for Carolyn — succumbed to whatever! So the female was left alone. Weeks later the female of a pair of long-tailed finches also departed her body. Carolyn told me that the female painted finch then spent quite a lot of time with the distressed long-tailed male finch, giving him support.

This seemed very unlikely to me with two very different species. But when I sat in the aviary watching them and observing, sure enough, the two birds were sitting almost touching in their common bond. Clearly, although not a pair — nor would they ever be — they were experiencing mutual benefits.

This is just one of the many aspects of Carolyn that I so enjoy and admire. She reminds me of the qualities of gentleness just in the way she lives, in the very energy of her Being. She freely shares her Love with the world . . . and I am blessed to be first in line!

CONTENTS

Contents

FOREWORD
By Linda Tellington-Jones, Ph.D

My entry into the secret life of nature occurred more than three decades ago as a result of an invitation from Michael to talk with an ancient Morton Bay Fig Tree, the same tree that inspired Michael's ground-breaking book, *Talking With Nature*.

I had journeyed to Michael's home at Bellingham, close to the eastern shores of Queensland, Australia, carrying a message I received while meditating in the heart of the Australian Outback, near the dusty settlement of Alice Springs.

I had spent the night before with a small group of spiritual explorers, on an all-night vigil on top of the giant red rock called Uluru, in a state of awe at the vastness of the galaxy and a breathtaking feeling of Oneness with the entire universe.

As I reached the desert floor after a hazardous descent down the 1,000-foot rock, I experienced an overpowering intuitive *knowing* that I must visit Michael to encourage him to write a book about his remarkable connection with Nature Spirits and his cooperation with kangaroos who had over-run his pasture lands.

I had learned to trust my intuition, no matter how strange it might seem, because of an astrological prophecy I had received for my thirtieth birthday. The prophecy stated that *"in my lifetime I would develop a form of communication that would spread around the world, and in order to do so I must learn to trust my Intuition."* Opening a Rosicrucian book in my husband's library, I found the definition of intuition as *Unlearned Knowledge*. I interpret that as the *direct knowing* that Michael describes in Chapter Four, a *knowing* we must learn to trust in order to become at One with Nature.

Learning to trust my intuition has been a cornerstone in my life ever since, and so I had no qualms about phoning Michael from Alice Springs and asking if I could come to deliver a message.

Michael and I had met for the first time the week before at the One Earth Gathering at the Brisbane Awareness Centre. During the week-long conference Michael shared riveting stories recalling mutual cooperation and agreements with kangaroos who had been over-running his pastures. Absolutely mesmerizing! Of even greater interest to me were his captivating encounters with fairy rings and fairy folk.

I had been enchanted by the Fairy Kingdom for many years. Until the Brisbane conference, however, my most beguiling experience was leading a small group of five-year-old children at the Esalen Institute on the wild Big Sur coast of California, on an adventure searching for fairies in the Esalen flower garden. It was a delightful exploration that yielded excited speculation, but no fairies revealed themselves that day.

That was about to change, however, at a gathering a world away. During the closing minutes of the conference I had an overpowering feeling that I must speak, before the crowd of a hundred international participants dispersed. I stood up spontaneously and asked if anyone was interested in joining me on a trip to the Brisbane Botanical Gardens to meditate in the hopes of having a fairy experience. A dozen hands shot into the air and we agreed to take the conference bus to the gardens.

I wish I had a photo of everyone who joined me that auspicious afternoon. As we sat down on the grass in a circle to meditate, I had a strong feeling that Nature Spirits were expecting us and I silently prayed for fairy energy to grace our circle.

Just seconds after I closed my eyes, two small figures appeared magically in the centre of our circle. A male and a female fairy — about eight inches tall — hovered at eye level. The male wore a shining crown with nine points. He remained in the middle of our circle, spinning in place. The rays of the late afternoon sun shone through the limbs of a magnificent Jacaranda tree, reflecting off the points of his crown, sending a beam of light into the heart of each person in the circle. The female fairy, carrying a tiny wand, flitted around the circle, touching each of us on the third eye, creating a transformative, magical, sparkle of light.

Waves of energy light up my cells and a smile of delight flushes my face as I recall those moments. I could barely contain my excitement those many years ago. The moment we finished the meditation I blurted out, "Who saw them?" Several acknowledged their presence, including Michael. It's curious that I don't remember more details but that propitious day opened new realms for me, which I attribute to Michael's influence.

One of my favourite chapters in this inspiring book you have in your hands (or on your screen!) is the fourth, where Michael paints a picture of the difference between left brain *knowledge* and right brain *knowing,* accentuating the necessity for trusting our inner knowing so that we may enter into the secret world of Nature. I am particularly taken with this chapter. *"Why?"* I hope you will ask. Because the right brain is also responsible for intuition, feeling and compassion, without which we cannot be fully human.

By the way, the prophecy that I would develop a form of communication that would spread around the world has been fulfilled. I am blessed to have birthed a gentle form of cell-to-cell and soul-to-soul bodywork and training exercises for animals and humans that is practiced on six continents. Known as Tellington TTouch®, the one-and-a-quarter circles are the foundation that awaken an inner re-membering of the Divine Spark in every cell in our bodies.

Michael's courage in speaking his truth and his genius at depicting the unseen realms of Nature has had a profound influence on my life and my work.

I began this foreword with the statement that my communication with the ancient Morton Bay Fig Tree on Michael's property was a turning point in my life — a gateway to a life-long love and respect for all the Kingdoms of Nature. Thank heaven I carefully wrote the exact words in my journal because parts of the message were entirely unfamiliar to me. It was only much later, when I shared the prophecy to large audiences, that I began to realize the propitious nature of the message and the impact it had on so many people.

The Message from the Morton Bay Fig Tree:

Once upon a time there were many like me. We had lived long upon this earth and had acquired much wisdom.

Our understanding and love sent out positive vibrations which had far reaching effects. Then came man with his lack of understanding.

The time of which I speak is not measurable in your mind.

The positive ions that were created by disruptive thoughts and actions caused disturbances to the delicate "Balance of Nature".

The negativity became so great that the entire planet was affected. That is what caused the actual axis imbalance of your planet. That is when the shift in axis occurred.

In order to re-balance or re-align the earth, your people must once again recognize the Kingdoms of the Plants, the Animals, the Minerals and the Nature Spirits as One with you and as vital to the survival of the Planet.

That your race recognizes the God within is only the start. That we are recognized as One with you is the key — not only to survival — but to Heaven On Earth.

At this critical time on the planet, when so many are disconnected from Nature, I believe this book holds a key that can unlock your innate connections for entrance into the secret world of Nature.

Enjoy the journey!   Blessings and Aloha from Hawaii,
Linda

Linda Tellington-Jones, Ph.D
Founder Tellington TTouch (R) Method
www.ttouch.com

ACKNOWLEDGEMENTS

WHILE I AM ALWAYS HAPPY to acknowledge those people who assist me during the process of writing a book, there are never many of them. I often read a book where the acknowledgements—which I always read—go on for several pages, with a bewildering number of people involved. I am almost, not quite, envious of them!

I am not a researcher. I simply live as consciously as I am able. I have found that when I am consciously in the moment and I need to know something, it triggers what I call direct knowing. In a more esoteric language this is known as mystical cognition. A deeper aspect of my consciousness connects with that which I need to know, and it becomes known to me. Notice that it is a need to know, never a wanting to know. Need and want express very different energies.

I find, as always, a need to thank my adorable wife, Carolyn. In truth, she is not my inspiration to write, this is built-in, but she does inspire the very best in me, and this also enters into my writing, as well as my regular public speaking. So by Carolyn being who she is, just the way she is, gives me a perfect reason to thank her for her contribution to my writing.

I sincerely thank my American publisher, Denise Williams of Six Degrees Publishing Group for making the whole process so deliciously easy. Goodbye to all the years of publishing struggles, and hello to publishing freedom. Any author will tell you the value of this!

To Brian and Theresa, our dear friends, thank you so very much for your expertise. Brian and Theresa Longhurst are English maestros of the written word. Brian takes a few of my beautifully constructed sentences and mutilates them into acceptable English. The odd thing is that after his treatment it reads so much better! And then there are all the comma things and colon things and semi-colon things; a bit like our own intestinal workings! Theresa takes these after I have placed them all perfectly, and after some very English juggling, makes it all look and read in a far better flow. Amazing!

I wish to thank my old friend Linda Tellington-Jones for her wonderful foreword. Linda was a great catalyst in my life when, many years ago she was visiting us. In those days I was frightened by what people would think of me if I spoke or wrote of fairies and elves, and suchlike. I kept it all hidden away. Linda was so open on the subject, and so utterly uncaring of what people might think of her, that it had a very liberating affect on me. I came out of the closet! Thank you, Linda, for this priceless gift.

Last, but not least, my thanks to my daughter, Tracey. Her help around our home, in ways far too numerous to recount, often enables me to have the uninterrupted hours I require for my writing.

To all the many and varied Beings of Nature who are in my life, and who will never read this — I know who you are — a vast, universal THANK YOU.

– Michael J. Roads

INTRODUCTION

H MM . . . ANOTHER BOOK! Will I ever stop this writing game? Would you believe that I wrote my best-selling *Talking with Nature* back in 1978? I had to endure many rejections before publisher H. J. Kramer finally took it — I was considered too far ahead of my time! — but thanks to Hal it was published in the U.S. in1985. *Journey into Nature* followed in 1987, enjoying a similar popularity. To be honest, it took about a decade for each book to reach the best-selling status, but they made it and are still in print all these years later as a single two-in-one book. Forty years have passed since I shared those early experiences, and now, with a much greater insight and far more experience I am ready to share more about the secret, and mostly unrealised, world of Nature, taking it to a new holistic level.

The purpose of this book is to teach you how to enter the secret world of Nature . . . if you so choose!

In my recent book, *From Illusion to Enlightenment*, I introduced my readers to the human aspect of the metaphysical world in which we live, or maybe, to state it more accurately, how to live in and experience the physical world from a greater metaphysical perspective.

Now it is the turn of Nature. What is the secret world of Nature, you might ask? Simply put, it is the metaphysical world. Interestingly, this is the true world, the world beyond all illusion. We live in the world of illusion attempting to understand it, all the while ignoring the true world around us that expresses in a greater reality.

In many ways this is an easier book to write, for Nature follows the blueprint of itself impeccably, whereas humanity has not only lost the blueprint of life, but has also lost the deeper knowing of ever having one!

Of course, there are exceptions to this; you may be one of them. I have read many books and listened to quite a number of people speaking about their relationships with Nature, oftentimes feeling doubt in what was written or spoken, other times rejoicing at their wonderful insights. We are living in times when there is a far greater acceptance of a broad spectrum communication with Nature . . . to our very great advantage. As you read these pages I suggest that you trust the whispers of acceptance in your heart rather than any mutterings of denial that may fester in your intellect. Being open to what is unknown to us is the way in which we grow. There is no growth in endlessly reinventing the wheel!

If you are one of my many readers who are just hanging-out waiting for my next book — I Love you folks! — well, here it is. You will have no doubts to overcome, no denial in the left-brain; just a river of familiar inner warmth and knowing in which to joyfully swim.

During the fifty years of my writing and public speaking career I have spoken and written much about the metaphysics of Nature. I may pull a few of those writings from my various other books into this one to illustrate a point that I am making, but it will only be a few. Obviously, my perspective of a mystical Nature has grown and expanded over the years, yet as I reread and remember some of my more dated experiences I am constantly surprised and impressed by their depths and insights. Truth is ageless.

In this book about Nature, Pan will be involved only in certain areas. By this I mean it is not a book sharing my constant interactions with Pan. Pan will only be involved when I clarify certain issues. I doubt that a moment of my life passes without the essence of Pan being with me . . . unfortunately this does not imply that I am always conscious of him. It is enough to say that Pan is a unique expression of an unfathomable energy of Intelligence. That I have any sort of relationship with this Loving vastness is enough. I am humbled, and overwhelmingly filled with gratitude that he is my mentor.

Like you, I too am growing. In my other books of a metaphysical Nature, Pan is the teacher and I am the student. In this book I am the teacher and hopefully, you are the student. Sure, many of my deeper insights came from Pan's unique guidance, but they also became my own experience. Nothing in this book is conjecture, theory, or speculation; it is all based in my own personal experience within the secret world of Nature.

I would like to recommend to my readers that you thoroughly immerse yourselves in my words about the structure of reality. It took me several years to be fully open and receptive to this, and it offers a very well explained shortcut for your deeper comprehension of the metaphysical world. For this, and other reasons, I humbly advise you to read and reread my second chapter very carefully. It will be of immense value to you as you realise how obvious it is that we all have this latent ability to enter the metaphysical world of Nature. Do not read it to evaluate and dissect, but to embrace and absorb. This will take trust, not in me . . . but in you!

Okay, having introduced you to this book, once again as in all my other books I will explain my altered terminology, my way of writing to communicate deeper meaning to you, the reader. As always in my books, I place a capital letter at the beginning of each word I wish to powerfully emphasise. Obviously there is a huge difference between transformational Change and a change of clothes! Or the Truth of Life and a truth that is personal. Or the Mystery of life that is beyond understanding, as distinct from an intellectual mystery. Or 'I Love my wife' and 'I love my car!' And so it goes.

— Michael J. Roads

Chapter One

REMINISCING

Everything is energy. We live our lives apparently contained within the borders and boundaries of physicality, and yet, paradoxically, we do not. This is an aspect of illusion. We see and experience all that which is apparent to us, yet there is so much more. And although on a certain level we actually experience this, we casually dismiss it without ever knowing what it is that we have so carelessly dismissed.

"Ah, that looks better," I said aloud. I sometimes talk to myself!

It certainly feels much better, came the unexpected silent reply. Surprised, I stopped in my tracks as I was walking past the bonsai on a corner of my garden pond.

Just a few days earlier, with my beautiful wife Carolyn, I had been to the outdoor wedding of a couple of good friends, and I had been impressed by a number of large bonsai *ficus* that had been strategically placed around the area of seating. The bonsai were really quite large, not at all traditional, and growing in various different containers ranging from large, shallow pots to big trays to very large convoluted slabs of wood.

Despite flaunting all the rules of bonsai — I like that — they were striking in their various eye-catching postures. *Look at us,* one of them said. I smilingly replied that I was, indeed, impressed by all of them. I had given them all a fairly close inspection while we waited for the lingering, chatting guests to gradually be seated.

Not unnaturally, the next day when I was admiring my own few bonsai, I found myself appraising their containers, wondering if I could improve on them, and how.

My bonsai of the *ficus* family are about forty to fifty years old. These days it amazes me that it is now so long ago that I took the tiny saplings and began their careers as bonsai. They all agreed to this, which is the only way that I operate. I also now have a few younger, strikingly colourful *bougainvilleas* as bonsai.

As I walked past them casting my eyes and feelings over them, it was rather like viewing old friends with the hidden intention of changing their place of habitation. They all knew exactly what I was up to, and strongly refused to cooperate in any such endeavour.

"Okay guys, I get the message, but are there no volunteers?"
We are willing.

Not unexpectedly, this response came from a couple of *banyan ficus* that I had bought just a few years earlier. They had never really powered away in the manner that my plants normally do, so I had been speculating on their future. In fact, I was hoping that they would be my volunteers.

I am the type of gardener who puts twisted, odd-shaped, old bush wood with potential aside, just in case the day comes when it will be needed. Grabbing two large pieces of such wood, I placed them artfully in a suitably large container pot, and lo and behold, it became a perfect artistic receptacle for my two *banyan ficus*, with their short, fat, almost deformed-looking trunks.

After they were both set in their new container, which offered them far more root room, and therefore growth, I placed them on the edge of my garden pond about a metre above the ground. Clearly approving, they seemed to glow with a new life expectancy. Me being me, they were proudly shown to Carolyn, happily getting her seal of approval. With this accomplished, their future was assured.

It was these ficus that I was admiring when they responded to my spoken aloud comment. I often wonder why it is that so many people have a problem with talking to plants. Animals, no problem . . . but plants! I can only assume that this is yet another of those self-imposed limits within the illusion.

Communication with Nature should be as much a part of our daily life as communicating with people, but it does require a few extra skills to be learned. Having said this, I need to emphasise how poorly we communicate with other people. We so very often tell lies and half-truths, we exaggerate and embellish, our energy is often deceitful and we all too easily speak the words designed to make us look good to other people. None of this works in the bigger picture. And . . . you need to be very clear that none of this will allow you any chance of a meaningful communication with Nature. There can be no hidden agenda. Communication is no more than a simple exchange of energy, but we are no longer a simple people; we are extremely complicated. Simple is powerful, but, I am sorry to say, as a people we are not focused in being powerful. We are scattered in our daily lives, quickly losing energy.

Everything is energy. We live our lives apparently contained within the borders and boundaries of physicality, and yet, paradoxically, we do not. This is an aspect of illusion. We see and experience all that which is apparent to us, yet there is so much more. And although on a certain level we actually experience this, we casually dismiss it without ever knowing what it is that we have so carelessly dismissed.

I could joke and say that if we dismiss it we don't miss it, but the reality is that we are left spiritually undernourished and impoverished by our overall lack of connection with Nature and our holistic world. Most people are isolated on the outside of life, struggling to look in. In this book I will explain how it is possible for people to *consciously* be on the inside, looking out! But, of course, this can only be a probability. You, the reader, will have to make your own choice about this . . . *and then live it*. If you do this, then the probability may become an actuality.

Although these days I am a spiritual teacher, there was a time when much of my public speaking was about the metaphysics of Nature, with a focus on plants. More and more people easily accept that we can have a two-way communication with plants, but the great majority of people still consider it both improbable and impossible. Despite this, these same people will talk to their cats and dogs without ever getting a reply, yet in some strange way this is more acceptable than talking to trees — whether extremely large or very, very small.

People still occasionally ask me, "So how do you communicate with trees, or even animals for that matter? I mean, how does it actually work?" I usually give a fairly brief reply, simply because the long answer is exactly that . . . far too long! However, I will give you, dear reader, the details that I usually omit when speaking about this subject.

I am sometimes asked if I communicate with Nature as much as I did at the time of writing *Talking with Nature* and *Journey into Nature*. The honest answer is no, I do not verbally communicate as much, but I *experience* more.

Looking back over my many years of communicating with Nature, I am aware of just how insecure I used to be in this process. It is rather like looking back to an entirely different person. I did not like many people in those early days, which was not to my advantage. In fact, from the time I began school I learned not to trust adults or even to truly like them. The school teachers we had in our harsh private school with their public thrashings in front of all the pupils, made this very easy. However, I did enjoy being with my schoolmates.

When I wrote *Talking with Nature* it was obvious to my many readers that Nature was my classroom as I struggled to accept that I could, indeed, communicate with Nature. And if I could, why couldn't other people? In my insecurity, I needed to be considered normal by others, yet that which I was experiencing was a living denial of 'normality'. People who know me today would have difficulty recognising the insecure me of those times. On one memorable occasion I was talking with a rubber tree (*ficus elastica)* and as it communicated with me, I felt ever more threatened and insecure. The tree then asked how I would feel if a hundred or a thousand other people could hear the same words. Would I end up trying to understand what these other people thought of such words? Would I feel happier and more secure with re-assurances from other people?

I knew that I would not. The journey to acceptance was my own.

Readers of *Talking with Nature* and *Journey into Nature* may re-member that they represented a time of major stretching and growing for me. In those days I could not even imagine my present relationship with a metaphysical Nature. I would like to say that I made rapid growth, but in truth I consider that I stumbled along, unwittingly clinging to my emotional insecurity for many years. I wanted a level of reassurance that I could not get, nor was it possible. But . . . over the years and far too many self-created traumatic experiences within the metaphysical world of Nature, I slowly grew and developed.

I am being this frank and honest simply because you may find yourself in a similar position one day — or, perhaps, already are. You can then think, *well, if Michael Roads was able to succeed, with all his doubts and insecurity, I know that I can*. And you are right, you can . . . if you persist. Avoid the unhealthy paths of cynicism and scepticism. These lead only to the prison of self-criticism.

As I look back over the years I marvel at how life always put me in the perfect place to learn my lessons. Not many people are blessed with living close to a beautiful river, yet high enough above it to always be out of range of the regular flood waters that accompany such rivers. Today I am aware that the place I *need* to be is always where I am. This also applies to you, dear reader, no matter where you are. When you genuinely *need* to move your location it will happen; *wanting* to move is not where your power lies. In the past I have tried several times to move from my current home. I no longer do this. When I married Carolyn, over ten years ago, it seemed logical and reasonable with a new wife to move to a new location, but it was not to be. No interest, no offers . . . and this for a large, very interesting home offering a really wonderful garden!

It taught me the perfection of imperfection. Of course, we live in a world where most people believe that nothing is perfect. I live in a world where I *know* that in a greater reality everything is breathtakingly perfect.

Where we are is perfect for both of us. This is where we are, where we both have the greatest potential for inner growth. I could easily say it is where we are *meant to be,* but this is such an overused New Age cliché. There is no meant to be. We are *where* we are; we are *who* we are; it *is* as it *is.* Meant to be is an intellectual concept based in logic and conjecture. People who wish to enter the secret world of Nature should never base their lessons in logic and conjecture. The problem with this is that Nature is neither logical nor is it reasonable to the self-limiting mind. It may surprise you to know that nothing in Nature is an intellectual expression.

You may be wondering why where I live is so perfect for both of us. The answer is that in some ways it can be so difficult and imperfect a place for us! Particularly me. As you may have surmised, I am a keen gardener. This is not my profession, it is my passion. Luckily my passion is also for life and living . . . so this includes everything I do; I am a passionate man! My garden is really my playground, but it is also my training arena where I am the one being trained. Unlike a horse in its arena, I do not trot in circles, but I do practice conscious gardening. I have written a book about this, *Conscious Gardening,* so enough said. One way of looking at the perfection of where we live is that in recent years, with our climate changes, we are having far too many droughts and there is seldom enough water. We have to catch and store all our rainwater from our roof, so a drought means not enough water. We are not on any local town water, so catching water in tanks and storing it is common in our district. In the early days I installed a lot of tanks, so I store a lot of water, around two hundred thousand litres . . . but this is not an endless supply.

Obviously, for a keen gardener this is not a perfect arrangement. However, the dichotomy of this is that it is also perfect. It has taught me to *see plenty where there is not enough.* I am learning to grow beyond the clutching hands of want, while deeply appreciating all that I have and for the bountiful water that is available. It has taught me to focus on the big wet event that is on its way, rather than grumbling about the big dry event that we are currently locked in. I have learned that this, too, will pass.

Nevertheless, I was recently quite shocked to learn that I had an old, unrecognised, long-term water poverty consciousness. Sure, I focussed on the big wet event to come, but I was emotionally caught by a parched and dried out garden as my various plants succumbed to the heat and the dry. This revealed my emotional attachment not so much to my plants, but to their wellbeing, to their natural growth during the summer months. And there was no growth during the long dry months of 2016, just endless hot days, strong sunshine — which I love — and nowhere near enough rain.

It was during late spring in 2017 that I finally saw my problem. I was shocked that I still had this attachment. A week later our very forthright friend and masseuse, the delightful Anita, pointed out to me that I had a poverty consciousness over water. She surprised me. Just in case I had not already received and connected with the required message, she delivered it once again. How good is that? She was right. Just a few days before she pointed this out, and knowing just how low our water tanks were, I had liberally watered various parts of the garden — something I never do. I had finally realised that I can buy *truckloads* of water — yes, it is costly — but I certainly have the money to buy it. So . . . what was my problem? I learned that emotional attachments can often blind you to the startlingly obvious.

Would you believe about a week after I watered various parts of a dried out and parched garden, an unexpected rain event came swiftly upon us, and it poured and poured with wonderful, blessed rain. For about a month we had an ongoing rain event that filled all our water tanks, and gave the garden a deep and thorough soaking. Truly, on the first day I danced in the rain, screaming out "Thank you. Thank you. Thank you." My lesson finally, finally learned, it would appear that I was rewarded. The new green growth in my revitalised garden and the surrounding bush (forest) was utterly amazing.

This is why where we live is perfect for us. I grew from this experience, and I continue to grow. It is not just the gardens that need to grow, but also the gardeners. Hence, the need to be a *conscious* gardener.

I earlier mentioned that I do not communicate with Nature as much as I used to. There are two factors to this: first, I now *experience* considerably more of a metaphysical Nature, with less of the talking: second, I took on the far more difficult task of communicating with people! Nature listens fully and impeccably to what I communicate, while people constantly translate my words into their own complex intellectual box of understanding, thereby reducing, altering or even erasing my meaning. Nature is always completely open, while so many people are fearfully closed. I guess I could keep going with this for a quite while! But it is enough to say that Nature *listens* with full consciousness, while people subconsciously only *hear* your words.

Summary: In this opening chapter I hope to have established that you will never know it all. There is always more to learn. While you live with a garden, or take walks in a natural wood, or forest, you will always be growing — so long as you do these things *consciously.* Just when you think you have a strong and certain insight into some aspect of Nature . . . it can change, grow, expand, becoming new and exciting. The intellect is inclined to hold fast to beliefs, knowledge and teachings, yet Nature is forever in constant flux and change. Certainly we may live lifetimes with little apparent change in how we view Nature, but hopefully, you will realise already that Nature is very much more than the physical form that we see and relate to.

Chapter Two

THE STRUCTURE OF REALITY

Realise also that this space-energy of humanity is not an exclusive;
it also includes everything in Nature . . . even the Earth itself is
energy. So, all humanity, all Nature our planet Earth, and our
whole solar system are energy, all sharing information. We might
as well take the final step and include the entire universe; all of
it is energy and all is continuously sharing information — but
nobody is listening. Okay . . . just a few. I listen. Any person who is
truly conscious and aware is able to listen.

We are going to dive deep in this chapter, for it is absolutely essential that you become aware of the whole fundamental principles of what we call life on Earth. We see, hear and experience only a fraction of life, and with this fraction we have deeply embedded and concretised our many and varied beliefs, doctrines, opinions and dogmas into the human psyche.

Please, open the mind and the heart before you dive in.

I would like to first remind you of just a few of the mind-boggling facts that physics and science now offer us. We are told that we see less than one percent of the electromagnetic spectrum, meaning that we see less than one percent of the greater reality of life. As if this is not limiting enough, we hear less than one percent of the audial spectrum, meaning that of all the vast range of sounds that surround us, we hear so very, very little. We are also told that the atoms in our bodies are 99.9999% empty space . . . but from my metaphysical perspective I would like to add that this space is not empty nothingness, it is energy. All energy carries information, and this energy is endlessly sharing information with all the energies of the universe.

Realise also that this space-energy of humanity is not an exclusive; it also includes everything in Nature . . . even the Earth itself is energy. So, all humanity, all Nature, our planet Earth, and our whole solar system are energy, all sharing information. We might as well take the final step and include the entire universe; all of it is energy and all is continuously sharing information — but nobody is listening. Okay . . . just a few. I listen. Any person who is truly conscious and aware is able to listen.

Everything that we see as physical is space, but the greater majority of it is beyond our visible spectrum of sight, so we see only the dense physical. From my metaphysical viewpoint, all of this space/energy is consciousness. This means that the consciousness of humanity, Nature, our planet, our solar system and our entire universe are all One consciousness. We often refer to this as Oneness!

Okay . . . this paves the way for further explanation.

In July 2015, at about two o'clock in the morning, I had an inner revelation about the structure of reality. Unfortunately it came into my sleeping consciousness and although on waking I tried for a couple of hours to bring it into thoughts and words in my aware consciousness, it eluded me. Because I am aware of the *timing* factor, I relaxed, knowing that the timing would arrive.

One August night in 2017, I woke up around the same time and the whole scenario of the structure of reality unfolded into my receptive and awake consciousness. For about a couple of hours I was receiving a higher education about the structure of reality, and the reality of structure. This continued until it was very clear in my conscious awareness. I realised that it was in perfect timing for this book, which, apart from the introduction, I had not yet begun. I love it when life excels itself!

I am going to do my best to explain this to you, for it is very appropriate, timely, and necessary for a deeper insight into, and experience of, Nature.

Okay . . . imagine a centrifuge into which is thrown many full shovels of various sized rocks, stones, gravel, numerous types of sand and soil, along with some water and ice. A concrete mixer is a good physical example, but imagine it spinning at a very great speed. As the centrifuge spins, all the rocks, stones and gravel and sand/soil particles, water and ice are thrown outward to their varying positions as determined by their weight and density. Now take away all outer limits to the centrifuge — let go of the cement mixer — increase to infinity the amount thrown into the centrifuge and everything in it will be propelled ever outward to reach its own outer limits in space. And this will vary greatly.

In your imagination, expand this centrifuge out until it is the size of our universe and spinning at the speed of light. Okay . . . now imagine a series of bandwidths from the outer limits to the inner centre of this immense universal centrifuge. There are literally thousands of these bandwidths from the outer limits of density to the very centre of Light. Just as with a radio we need to know the bandwidth to be able to tune into a certain station, so these cosmic bandwidths indicate the reality of structure and the structure of reality via their frequency density. Obviously, all similar densities end up in the same bandwidth. These bandwidths are often referred to as parallel universes, for they all occupy the same apparent space, while appearing to be parallel to us.

You will probably not be surprised to learn that our three-dimensional physical density bandwidth is close to, but not fully at, the outer limits of this vast, universal centrifuge. Now, however, the explanation becomes a bit more complex. In Truth we are metaphysical souls, and as such our energy is very light, not at all dense, yet our experience is of living our three-dimensional lives in physical bodies. Unfortunately, we have taken on the limits of this density even though it does not represent the truth of who of we are. To make matters even worse, we do not live our lives as a light-soul in the dense-physical; we live our lives as a dense-physical in our physical density.

As we look at, and experience the world around us in and from our dense physical reality, we are unable to see the structure of reality on other bandwidths, for they are beyond our frequency spectrum of sight and sound — even though they occupy the same space! Over aeons of time we have taken on the belief that we are physical Beings, living within our limits as though we are living life fully. As becomes obvious, we are only living a fraction of the potential of our true, metaphysical soul reality. To make the situation even more clear, we are physically three-dimensional while all the expressions of our mental, intuitive, and emotional bodies are four-dimensional . . . and yet we continue our lives within the confines and restrictions of living our self-imposed perceptual limits!

Let me present it another way. These are a few of our bodies:

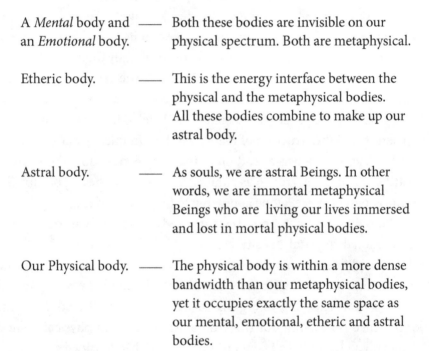

A *Mental* body and —— Both these bodies are invisible on our
an *Emotional* body. physical spectrum. Both are metaphysical.

Etheric body. —— This is the energy interface between the
physical and the metaphysical bodies.
All these bodies combine to make up our
astral body.

Astral body. —— As souls, we are astral Beings. In other
words, we are immortal metaphysical
Beings who are living our lives immersed
and lost in mortal physical bodies.

Our Physical body. —— The physical body is within a more dense
bandwidth than our metaphysical bodies,
yet it occupies exactly the same space as
our mental, emotional, etheric and astral
bodies.

When I travel metaphysically, I move my focus of Self away from the physical body into my Light-body. Light-body is my name for the mental, emotional and etheric bodies that make the astral body.

However, I am awake and conscious when I do this, not asleep. The astral body of everyone moves away from the physical body in deep, rapid eye movement (REM) sleep. If this were to suddenly not happen, there would quickly be mass insanity.

Okay, let us now return to the bandwidths. Just as the outer bandwidth is first and second dimensional, the next is our familiar third and fourth dimensions, then the fifth and sixth dimensions and so on — although we quickly reach a point where dimensions cease to have any meaning to us. Every bandwidth has its own frequency: the higher the frequency the greater is the expression of the reality of structure and the more complex the structure of reality to experience life. It gets even more fascinating when you realise that every bandwidth occupies the same place in space. Actually, it occupies the moment, rather than space, but we so seldom experience the fullness of life in the moment that we have become addicted to linear time and space.

At this point you may be thinking, "What's he talking about with our third and fourth dimension?" So let me explain once again: We are physically three-dimensional, but metaphysically, we are fourth-dimensional. All our thoughts, our emotions, feelings, intuition, imagination, etcetera, are obviously not physical; they are metaphysical and express on a fourth dimensional reality. It should be noted and remembered that the metaphysical always precedes the physical.

The view of our solar system from our third- fourth-dimensional viewpoint is totally different from the view in a fifth- sixth-dimensional reality . . . and so on. We experience so-called space and distance and connect it with linear time, giving us our self-limited three-dimensional reality. Like you, I see this physically, but when I move into a fifth-dimensional reality in my Light-body, I see it very differently: there is no space and distance, and all time occupies the same moment. This is when you are able to begin to experience and comprehend the greater reality of what we call God — a God that we have rendered in our own image and reduced to fit in our very limited third- fourth-dimensional conceptual understanding.

13

Starting from close to the outer, most dense bandwidth, and moving inward, our comprehension of the universe increases exponentially — that is, if we like to metaphysically undertake the journey. And comprehension is rather different from understanding. Understanding is based in the intellect, while comprehension is based in our intelligence. I comprehend much that I do not understand, nor do I need to. We have turned understanding into a hurdle, for it represents the dense level frequency of structure attempting to understand a higher frequency level of structure, and this is not possible. However, if you move your higher metaphysical frequency into the higher frequency of the structure you are attempting to understand, you will then experience and quite easily comprehend the greater reality of it.

In our metaphysical body, we have seven basic chakras affecting the physical body and five chakras affecting the metaphysical body. A chakra is a spinning wheel of light/colour energy. Even if you are familiar with this, maybe I can give you further insight into what this means: The first seven chakras connect you with the physical world, with Nature, with the elements and the elementals.

Red base chakra connects you with earth.
Orange sacral chakra connects you with water.
Yellow solar plexus chakra connects you with fire.
Green heart chakra connects you with air.
Blue throat chakra connects you with the etheric.
Indigo brow chakra connects you with universal wisdom.
Violet crown chakra connects you with a greater reality.

The next five chakras all connect the metaphysical you with the essence of a much higher frequency spectrum/bandwidth:

The ultra-violet eighth chakra connects you *with your higher spiritual potential, offering illumination and higher communication.*

The rainbow colours of your ninth chakra connects you *with the blueprint of the soul you are through your many incarnations/lives.*

14

The pure light energy of your tenth chakra connects you *with your divine creativity and the synchronicity of life.*

The brilliant rose light of your eleventh chakra connects you *with Self in other dimensions and realities of the higher spectrum.*

The intense blazing miniature sun of your twelfth chakra connects you *with the vast metaphysical universe to which you can now listen, and experience.*

I need to add that none of these chakras open automatically. As you grow in consciousness, so the chakras develop and open. The higher chakras need to be consciously opened to be experienced. This is a natural process of conscious evolution in the growth of a human Being.

> *Caution:* Never, I repeat, *never* get involved with people who claim to open chakras. This is seriously unnatural and metaphysically damaging. A very dangerous practice.

At my 5-Day Intensives I teach people how they can develop and open their chakras. This promotes conscious spiritual growth which in turn raises a person's frequency, opening them to, and connecting them with, higher and finer bandwidths.

All these bandwidths of universal life suggest that, whether we live it or not, we have the capacity and potential of living as multidimensional Beings. What a paradox; the incredible diversity beyond our sight and sound is as close to us as our breath, yet as far away from our experience as the furthest star and our unshakeable belief in separation.

Finally, maybe now you will have a better comprehension of Pan. Pan means 'all'. Pan occupies every bandwidth simultaneously. Pan is an ancient, vast conscious Intelligence that occupies all the frequencies of the infinite spectrum. Even I, for the first time, have a better comprehension of the very magnitude of Pan. It is very humbling, but never reducing.

I will do my best to introduce you to the metaphysical world of Nature. We all easily see the physical bandwidth of Nature and thus we are inclined to believe that Nature is purely physical, just as we believe ourselves to be, but it is not so. The bandwidth of a metaphysical Nature is sharing the same space/moment as the physical form, but on a much higher frequency. This is where our *deeper* connection with Nature takes place.

Summary: Hopefully I have established here a whole new threshold on which to stand as you begin to open the door to the secret world of Nature.

You are now aware of the full potential spectrum of the amazing Being whom you truly are. You grow this Being, not with intellectual fodder for the brain, but by consciously focusing on those chakras and moving through them from Base to the Twelfth chakra with your conscious imagination. If you can visualise them as you do this, so well and good, but it is not an absolute necessity. Just by doing this consciously, maybe once a day, or week — it depends on you — you will grow in consciousness. This *is* soul development.

Chapter Three

ON LISTENING

Listening is very different from hearing. You need to be fully consciousness to listen, not subconscious. You can hear and think, but you cannot listen and think. And most people are thinking nonstop throughout a conversation. They hear the words, but they are never listening to them for they are busy thinking about an agreeable or argumentative answer. And this most often happens to all the people in the conversation, unrealised, unknowing. If you consciously listen to a person you metaphysically connect with them. If they lie to you, instantly you energetically know. When you only hear a person speaking there is no deeper connection; they can lie and you may never know.

A person who believes self to be separate from all life because this is what their five senses tell them, is a person living and lost in illusion. In this illusion the basic forms of communication are spoken words, art — mostly in the form of pictures — and the sounds of music. All this is energy, comprising our normal manner and various other means of communication, but it falls far short of our greater potential.

Sound is very much a part of our world. It would seem to me that, like monkeys, we are often a rather noisy, clamorous species. For many this is a comforting factor, for sound, or noise, gives them a form of connection with their environment. Other people shun cities and their noise, preferring the peace and quiet that should be found in the countryside. Because of the way we each develop our own relationship with sound, we are unwittingly creating our relationship with life. Unknowingly, we are also determining our inner growth in consciousness, or our lack of it.

Consider the many people who have a TV or radio on to give them a background noise; do they really listen to it? They use it to take away any possible silence. For many people silence is threatening, although most of them would deny this. They would say, and fairly so, that the background sound is company. Then there are the many people who have an iPod almost glued into their ears, with the choice of hundreds of sound tracks. I am sure they do listen to some of it, but when they are driving, or out walking with the iPod in place, or in a brief, often hurried conversation, they are not truly listening. And sadly, many people who are *without* an iPod in a conversation do not truly listen to the other person either. But I will explain this and how it affects our relationship with a metaphysical Nature.

I am pointing to just a few of the more obvious reasons of why people, living in a sound-soaked environment, do not listen. It is a lost ability. There is also a belief involved in this. People believe that if they can hear a person talking, then they are listening to them. Nothing could be further from the truth. To hear a person talking is one thing (most people can do this) but to *listen* to a person talking is something else altogether. Very few everyday people actually do this, or even *can* do it! Interestingly, most psychiatrists and psychologists are taught to *actively* listen to their patients. This would be a very beneficial practice if it were taught in schools.

We live in a world of ever-increasing deafness. Some of it is age re-lated, much is due to industrial noise and general noise pollution, some is genetic . . . there are many different physical reasons. One reason that is never investigated is the metaphysical reason: *we do not listen.* When we truly *listen* we make a metaphysical connection with whom, or what, we are listening to. When we only *hear* the sounds of music or voices, that metaphysical connection is absent. A true musician con-nects with their music. The conductor of an orchestra absolutely listens to the music of the orchestra as a whole, and to each of the individual players. Orchestral conductors have perfected true listening . . . maybe without ever realising it!

I also suffer from a degree of deafness. I grew up on a very mechanised farm in an age of ignorance regarding the wisdom of ear-protectors and efficient sound insulation. Now, in my mature years, I definitely suffer due to the constant noises generated during those long-ago winter months of working alongside the loud, noisy, roaring of the grain dryers, simultaneous with the loud swishing noise of grain turning over and over in the all-steel seed-dressing machines. Plus, there were the months of tractor driving, all with no ear protection. It was all loud, deafening noise. At the time it seemed to be no problem at all . . . but, as with so many others, I now pay the price with diminished hearing.

Also, I confess, I did not truly listen to anyone. Not at school nor at home. I would forget what was said almost as soon as the words were spoken. I was hearing the words, but I most certainly was not listening.

I hope I have established for you that there is a significant difference between hearing and listening. Hearing is a subconscious action. It does not require any focus or concentration . . . unless you suffer deafness. If there is a sound near you, then you hear it. If, during an interesting conversation, a dog starts barking, you will hear the dog whether you like it or not. Hearing is not selective. You will have to stop the dog barking to continue clearly hearing the other person with no impediment.

Listening is very different: it *is* selective. You need to be fully conscious to listen, not subconscious. *You can hear and think, but you cannot listen and think.* And most people are thinking nonstop throughout a conversation. They hear the words, but they are seldom, or mostly not listening to them, as they are busy thinking about an agreeable or argumentative answer. And this is happening to all the people in the conversation, unrealised, unknowing. If you consciously listen to a person, you metaphysically connect with them. If they lie to you, you will instantly, energetically, know. When you only hear a person speaking, there is no deeper connection; they can lie and you may never know.

Seriously, who ever listens to the politicians blathering on and on? So when they speak their litanies of lies, no one is listening, we just hear the words. It goes even deeper than this. The left-hemisphere of the brain hears the words and has an ongoing conversation with them — thoughts — but it is unable to listen. Listening comes from the right-hemisphere of the brain, or the whole-brain person. The left-brain is busy organising the incoming words to be met by the — often opposing — outgoing words. The right-brain simply embraces them . . . and deeply *knows* their holistic meaning.

If during a conversation, the mind wanders and you lose some of the conversation, the left-brain will automatically fill in the missing words based on the context of what has been said, or what you *thought* they said. And, mostly all unrealised. Lost in your own thoughts, you often do not realise that you have wandered out of a conversation, even though you may be aware of rejoining it. We all do it, frequently. When we are introduced to a group of people, or just a couple, most of us forget the names within minutes. We were not listening. We shook hands, but we made no *conscious* connection.

I am belabouring our communication with each other — or should I say *lack* of it — because I want you to realise that if we are unable to have more than a superficial communication with each other, how can we expect to communicate with Nature where words, as such, are useless?

I hope this is giving you pause for thought. I am really only scratching the surface of this, but your desire to communicate and more deeply connect with the metaphysical world of Nature has no chance at all if you are unable to *consciously* listen. I cannot overemphasise the value and importance of this. I have over fifty years of active experience behind these words.

I often smile during one of my Intensives when a person remarks to me that they are shocked to discover that they can hold their breath longer than they can stop thinking. Try it. You may get a surprise! Most people are thinking at around two to three hundreds words a minute. And most of these thoughts are just recycled nonsense . . . meaning, *no sense*. Even more scary is the realisation that the stress levels of the emotional and mental content of this nonsensical thought is very similar to how it was a thousand incarnations ago. Sure . . . different languages, different words, different meanings . . . but the same anxieties, same stresses, same worries. Different causes, certainly, but the same values apply. Stress is stress, no matter the cause or historical period.

Why am I so strongly emphasising this?

You will be aware that very few people truly communicate with animals. People like the long-established Linda Tellington Jones, also Penelope Smith, and the more recent and brilliant Anna Breytenbach, to name a few whom I personally know, plus an increasing number of others who have undoubtedly developed this talent — and probably numerous other people who are not publicly known — are all comparatively rare people. When any of us communicate with the various forms of Nature, be it animal or mountain or tree or river, we mostly do it in silence. We are the ones who translate the *energy* of the silent communication into words. To do this, several factors are involved, but first among them is the ability to be still, silent . . . and listen.

Nature communicates only in the moment. Only the moment is reality. The past and the future are illusion. Only humans play their games in the world of illusion. Nature lives and expresses in the world of reality. It becomes obvious therefore, that for us to communicate or deeply connect with Nature, we have to leave the world of illusion and join the world of reality. And if at this stage you may think that I am exaggerating, then your quest to connect with Nature is in big trouble.

When you think, you think your way out of the moment and into illusion. When you are listening — no thoughts — then you are fully in the moment. You are in the *real* world. Mind you, this happens to humans very rarely! This indicates that you listen your way *into* the moment, and you think your way *out* of it. Take a deep breath . . . and listen!

Listening is one of the most powerful abilities you can develop for your overall benefit. The repercussions reach far beyond any communication with Nature. All life exists and expresses in the moment. Nothing in Nature ever leaves the conscious moment. We are seldom in it. Nothing in Nature thinks. We seldom stop. In the immediate moment is whatever or however you perceive God. In the immediate moment there is unconditional Love, peace beyond understanding, soul-joy, conscious intelligence, absolute freedom. All these exist in the immediate moment, yet pilgrims and spiritual seekers travel the outer world looking for them. All exist in the immediate moment, closer than the seeker's breath and yet a billion miles away when the seeker peers through the murky blindfold of the intellect.

I learned to listen many years ago. I used to live very close to the Bellinger River in New South Wales — a river I loved. For five years, I would sit on an old, thick bridge-board suspended over the water, and I would attempt to listen to the river. At times it would be a few hours a day, often a solitary hour, other times a few minutes a day. It depended on the weather, my schedules, and my moods. One year passed, then another, and all I heard was the mocking sound of my own stupid useless thoughts as I tried to stifle them. I heard traffic sounds, dogs barking, tractors in the fields on the other side of the river, people shouting, children laughing. You name it, I probably heard it . . . but never did I hear silence. I heard the river chuckling and gurgling over the riverbed, and the sullen noises it made when in flood, forcing trees and riverbanks to collapse into its turgid, surging, implacable water.

All I wanted was to listen to the deep, inner silence of the river. I knew it was there. I knew this with a deep, intuitive conviction. Eventually, of course, I made a breakthrough. The river, however, was a strict teacher. One time I went down to my place on the old bridge-board, and a diesel engine was running full blast on the opposite side of the small river. It had been put there overnight, and was pumping water to irrigate a large field of potatoes. The noise was deafening, horrible. I hated it. As a result, I walked down the river until the irrigation pump was but a distant murmur. When I sat down to listen, I muttered, "Ah . . . that's better."

The river spoke to me.

How do you expect to learn to listen if you cringe away from sound?

"It's too distracting," I replied. "How can anyone listen in all that noise?"

The pump is there for your benefit. You ignore the sound and listen to the silence. Sound requires outer hearing. Silence requires inner listening. Both are very different. Sitting here will seriously delay the project.

With a deep sigh of despair, I went back to my bridge-board, and sitting in the overwhelming noise of the engine, I did my best to listen.

You will smile when you learn that it was within the blasted noise of that pump engine that I eventually was able to listen. It was curious. My physical ears could hear the noise, but as I learned to listen into ever deepening levels of inner silence, it was as though the engine noise was receding into the background until it was no more than a loud murmur. It was all about focus. It was so easy to focus on the sound and oppose it, and it was so difficult to focus on the silence and be with it. But I persisted . . . and it happened. This was probably halfway through the fifth year of practicing.

Weeks after my breakthrough, flood waters, that six years earlier had delivered my bridge board, now swept it away. My time was finished. Just another six weeks later and life took me away from that river forever.

Or did it?

Before I left to go from New South Wales to Queensland, I sat down by the river, thanking it for being such a brilliant teacher. Moments later, as we sat in companionable silence, the metaphysical river began to flow through me, while the physical river continued flowing smoothly between its beautiful green riverbanks. The energy of the metaphysical river flowed through me when I eventually got to my feet and left; it continued to flow me when I moved to Queensland, and it is flowing through me now as I sit writing these words.

This is the metaphysical world of Nature that I so Love.

Summary: We have now established that Nature is a unique teacher, but also that we are resistant to actually *being* taught. In our so-called civilised society we have deep-seated issues, believing that we are somehow above and beyond Nature. Nothing could be further from the truth. Learning to listen makes a great power available to you — the power of Now.

Listening is not about simply hearing physical words or sounds, they are often a nuisance; listening is a *surrender* to the moment with a quiet mind and an open heart. We are almost never in this place. We live in the illusionary world of subconscious thoughts with a full and busy mind. And sadly, a heart that is all too often closed to self/Self. Honour yourself by learning to truly listen.

Chapter Four

ABOUT THE BRAIN

Connecting and communicating with any form of Nature — all is One — requires that we express from knowing rather than from the speculation of knowledge. The left-brain thrives on knowledge, while the right-brain thrives on knowing. Okay, what is the difference? Knowledge has a 'use-by' date, even though the left-brain denies this. Knowledge is always in the past, while knowing is only in the moment. Knowledge is based on information and calculation, while knowing is based in the moment of intuitive insight. Never trust your intuition, says the left-brain, too unreliable, too fanciful, too prone to errors; you need to prove this intuitive insight with researched scientific facts. Hmm . . . I guess you have to decide which world you want to live in. The world of connection, trust and Oneness, or the world of isolated, but so-called proven facts. The problem is that Nature has no left-brain intellect, but it does have consciousness, and this consciousness never leaves the moment — the place of knowing. This is the expression of conscious intelligence. And, dare I say it, very right-brain!

I am aware that interspecies communication is now coming into its time. More and more people are interested in developing this skill, and it will grow. I consider it important to steer such people along a path of truth, rather than a path of conjecture and intellectual misrepresentation and misinterpretation.

Only today I read the headline to an article and its accompanying YouTube that was very misleading and false. It was words to the effect that 'people are learning to listen to the thoughts' of animals. This is so blatantly incorrect that it disturbed me. I became sensitive to the fact that I, too, could be careless with my words. Again, it was perfect, because the intellectual assumption in that article was a forewarning for me not to make the same error. Mind you, there is no blame attached here; the writer is quite probably convinced of the veracity of their words.

To me, this is a left-brain problem. The left-brain needs to understand its subject to be able to proceed, or at the very least to have an intellectual avenue down which it can progress. But it so happens that the left-brain is not equipped for interspecies communication. It is better equipped for fear and survival — for producing and accelerating anger and aggression, for human fight, flight, or freeze. It is logical, reasoning, and argumentative. It is also about language, articulation, mathematics and our many mental skills, along with other hugely important factors in our everyday life.

Please, do not read into this a criticism of the left-brain hemisphere, because none is implied. I am simply stating that our left-brain activity is now very dominant in the Western World, along with the Asian countries. If this suggests that left-brain dominance is partially economically driven, there is truth in that. However, in our Third World countries the left-brain is also dominant. This would suggest that perhaps the greatest factor in left-brain dominance is that *subconsciously* the intellect tends to cling to more-of-the-same, no matter what the cultural circumstances. It is estimated that approximately 85% of modern people are left-brain dominant. Probably another reason for this is that our whole educational system is based in the left-brain intellect. The few exceptions are a small number of aware, holistic, private schools — the Rudolph Steiner Schools, the Waldorf Schools, for example, all of which add up to a mere fraction of the overall educational system.

The left-brain can intellectualise a cause and reason for war. It is as unreasonable as it can be reasonable. It particularly likes it if other people fight the battles that it sees as logical, right, and conclusive. The left-brain cannot relate to being wrong. While it holds the historical information that wars cause an escalation of wars, the left-brain actually believes that you can fight for peace — despite all evidence to the contrary. The left-brain cannot relate to the fact that a country and its people not at war is by no means indicative of that country and its people living in peace. They are simply a country not at war with another country. The people's personal self-hate, enmities, anger, family quarrels, fights and everyday mini-wars continue.

The left-brain can be profoundly clever, yet it can also be just as profoundly stupid. Just watch the TV World News one night. I rest my case!

Okay, if I have put you off the idea that animal communication is, or can be a function of the intellectual left-brain . . . wonderful!

Those few — around 15% of the global population who are mainly right-brain dominant and naturally whole-brain balanced — may often find themselves disadvantaged by the way our modern society functions. To be accurate, the small percentage of whole-brainers do well in any environment; they are naturally balanced, usually more open and mostly more in harmony with life. Unfortunately, the right-brainers *really* struggle in a left-brain dominant world.

It is a *very* left-brain dominant world right now. As a species we are more disconnected from Nature than we have ever been. Dominant, the left-brain alone cannot make the Nature connection; it requires the whole-brain in harmony and balance to do this. I have discussed this with Anna Breytenbach, and we laughed as we both shared experiences of people we were teaching who attempted to force communication with Nature via the intellect. It does not work this way. Seriously . . . a tree has no intellect, nor does a black leopard named Spirit! But they both have conscious intelligence . . . and they both know how to brilliantly communicate energetically. Anna told me that her first lesson in her workshops on animal communication is about physics. She said that many people found this disconcerting. I chuckled and told her that in my spiritually-based Intensives, I, too, quite often begin with quantum physics. Of course, what we are both actually talking about is . . . energy!

The right-brain has a very different function from the left-brain. There is no better or worse, or right or wrong, or should or shouldn't with our brain functions . . . it is all about balance. We all have both hemispheres, but dominance is the problem, whether it be left or right brain. I was born right-brain dominant. Left-brain school was such a totally bewildering experience for me that I basically closed down. I was in the bottom-of-the-class cluster of four or five kids all my school life, which only lasted for nine years. I left school at fourteen. The day I left was when I knew there is a God!

With a brilliant, left-brain dominant brother who excelled at school, my father unkindly judged me as incompetent. The fact that at the age of ten I had a thriving collection of over two-hundred cactus and tropical plants, of which I knew all their Latin names and culture, completely passed him by. In my later years, as I reflect back on this, I note that he had cause to rethink his early judgements of me and attempted to make amends before he died in his early sixties. That was good for both of us!

I have had to learn to balance my brain. I consider today that, although I am still right-brain dominant, I operate more from a whole-brain per-spective. The reason I am writing about brain dominance is very simple. For you to communicate and/or truly connect with Nature requires that you have a balanced whole-brain function. Literally, your whole ener-gy-field is affected by this.

I have a list I compiled of about forty-five differences between the left-brain and right-brain functions. I will share just a few to give em-phasis to my point about the problem with left-brain dominance con-necting with Nature.[1]

Left-brain	Right-brain
what we think	*what we feel*
mortal personal-self	*immortal soul-self*
isolation and separation	*connection and Oneness*
constant mind chatter	*inner peace and quiet*
intellectual and clever	*intelligent and wise*
good, bad, right, wrong	*it is as it is*
competition	*cooperation*
head knowledge	*heart knowing*
the physical	*the metaphysical*
more subconscious	*more conscious*

This is enough to illustrate my point that left-brain dominance is very ill-equipped for connecting with Nature, while equally indicating that the skills we need are already available within our right-brain capabilities.

I will offer you a number of pointers that the right-brain hemisphere will immediately *get*. The left-brain may be more inclined to disagree, or *not* get it. I do not want to use the word, *understand*, because this is a strongly left-brain function. It needs to understand . . . and how do you understand that a tree with no intellect is able to communicate with you? The right-brain instantly *gets* it; it *comprehends* without the need to understand. It is rather like the right-brain listening to music . . . it *connects* in a holistic way. This means that the musician is able to *play by ear*, easily picking up and repeating some music it heard with which it connected. The left-brain musician can hear and enjoy the music, but to play it the person needs to read from the musical score. They need to learn the music, while the right-brain musician only needs to hear it. Of course, this is only a generalisation to make my point.

I consider that the greatest obstacle to the dominant left-brain in connecting with Nature is the incessant chatter of words. There are two layers to this: 1. The conscious thoughts of deliberate, aware cogitation of a problem or situation; 2. The deeper level of repetitive, subconscious thoughts that the thinker is not even aware of thinking.

When I retreated upriver to get away from the irrigation pump, I was very aware of my thoughts as I mentally raged against the noise that had driven me away. On a deeper energetic level, I was far noisier than the pump! This increased my despair as I, the inner noise maker, was seeking inner silence. When, after months of inner conflict, I finally surrendered to the loud noise of the irrigation pump . . . I found the inner silence!

If I say that silence is within, never to be found on the outer, the right-brain agrees enthusiastically, but the left-brain needs to think about it. Such a statement is not logical; it does not make sense. Conclusion: reject statement.

To make matters worse, if I say that the Nature that is surrounding you is within the human consciousness, the right-brain rejoices at such insight. The more volatile left-brain reacts and rejects. If I see Nature outside of myself, as I do — then this information must be false, it thinks. The difference is that the left-brain organises information while the right-brain embraces it. The results of these two very differing ways of dealing with information lead to often startlingly divergent outcomes. There is no right or wrong to the workings of either hemisphere of the brain, I am simply illustrating their different modes of relating to life. The intellect has developed in the left-brain, while the more holistic aspect of the right-brain hemisphere nurtures intelligence. Together, as One, the whole brain can celebrate a wonderful, fulfilling life.

Yet another aspect of the hemispheres is rather dissimilar. The left-brain is impatient, and as you probably guessed, patience is within the right-brain. And we all know that we live in a world of increasingly aggressive and impatient people. Road rage! Who had heard of this twenty years ago? There is nothing quite like congested city traffic to indicate the way a drivers brain works and which hemisphere is dominant when under pressure!

Can you imagine getting impatient with an incomprehensible and unfathomable metaphysical Nature? I've done it, and it does not work! Oddly, the right-brain is aware that it is *already connected* to this aspect of Nature, just as it knows that no *physical* connection is necessary. The right-brain is amazingly patient simply because it has no relationship with linear time. Its relationship is with metaphysical, spherical time, where all time occupies the same moment. The left-brain, however, deeply relates to linear time, knowing and experiencing no other. It would scoff at the very idea that all time occupies the same moment, because it has no metaphysical relationship with time, or life. Nature lives in two different time zones, just as we do. Whereas we, with our left-brain dominance relate only to linear time, Nature, although physical and biological, relates only to all time occupying the same moment.

Before I leave this subject, I will detail one other aspect. Nature is both physical and metaphysical . . . as are we. Nature is so powerfully aware of itself as immortal and metaphysical that it has considerably less regard for its transient physical expression. We humans have so much regard for the wellbeing of the physical and mortal aspect of ourselves that we have almost zero relationship with our metaphysical and immortal selves. And yet, surely perversely, it is our *disregard* for our wellbeing that underlies most of our sickness and ill health. We certainly are complex creatures!

Connecting and communicating with any form of Nature — all Nature is One — requires that we express from *knowing* rather than from the speculation of knowledge. The left-brain thrives on knowledge, while the right-brain thrives on knowing. What is the difference? Knowledge has a use-by date, even though the left-brain denies this. Knowledge is always in the past, while knowing is only in the moment. Knowledge is based on information and calculation, while knowing is based in the moment of intuitive insight. Never trust your intuition, says the left-brain, too unreliable, too fanciful, too prone to errors; you need to prove this intuitive insight with researched scientific facts.

Hmm . . . I guess you have to decide which world you want to live in. The world of connection, trust and Oneness, or the world of isolated, but so-called proven facts. The problem is that Nature has no left-brain intellect, but it has consciousness, and this consciousness never leaves the moment — the *place of knowing*. This is the expression of conscious intelligence. And, dare I say it, very right-brain!

Summary: We have now established that there is no intellectual left-brain way of truly connecting with the secret world of Nature. We need to be conscious, aware and open, without a brain full of beliefs and techniques. We need to cultivate and increase our engaging with right-brain, developing a far more balanced approach not only to Nature, but to our whole life.

---

1. To increase right-brain activity, choose which works best for you, *and do it*. Singing for enjoyment . . . laughter yoga . . . still mind, silent walking in Nature . . . conscious gardening . . . simple fun . . . poetry . . . simple day-dreaming . . . reading fantasy . . . playing with children . . . conscious mental relaxation . . . smelling flowers . . . stroking animals. And now, the **big** ones: trusting self . . . being aware of being conscious . . . smiling at people and meaning it . . . consciously choosing Love and *expressing* it!

Chapter Five

NATURE . . . THE UNIVERSAL TEACHER

With the left-brain viewing the world and life as outside of itself, it is natural enough that we have become onlookers of Nature, rarely participants. Very few people realise and/or experience life as an inside-of-Self process. We look through our eyes at the collective belief illusion of the world around us, and for us, that is life. This is where we can learn so much from Nature. Nature has almost the opposite experience of life. Nature is a total participant in life, never an onlooker.

Nature has so much to teach us. It would take a book on its own to just cover the agricultural and horticultural aspects alone, but that is not for me to write here. Here I am content just to summarise some of the lessons from Nature that are generally overlooked in our busy left-brain dominant world of today.

Today, most people are becoming aware that we pay a high price for our escalating disconnection from Nature. It is obvious that people become ever more spiritually and materially impoverished by working against Nature. Our food becomes ever more depleted as GM flourishes. Our modern farmers become ever more isolated and diminished by their increasing disconnection from the living soil, which, in turn, becomes the impoverishment of the consumers of their produce . . . Oneness! Happily, we have ever-increasing numbers of eco farmers, biological farmers, organic farmers, and their like. We also have eco-oriented organisations to disseminate new health and wellbeing information to the public; all this is to our benefit. Even some of the giant supermarkets are now offering organic products as they follow the trends . . . or perhaps the money! But, despite this positive organic aspect, it represents only a tiny, (but happily, expanding) fraction of the food consumed by a basically indifferent, uncaring majority proportion of humanity. To add to the craziness is the startling revelation that while a third of the world starves, half of all the food that is produced in the Western World is thrown away. The throw-away king of trade is the use-by date stamped onto all our food. This is inflicted on the food manufactures by the insurance companies to ensure that nobody can make a claim on spoiled food outside the use-by date.

We are *all* spiritually impoverished by the way the majority of humanity so casually trashes Nature. Take, for an example, some of the councils in suburban areas that spray a one metre area around the base of electricity poles and road signs with Roundup, or Zero. Because of its highly toxic carcinogenic glyphosate content, it is sickness waiting to happen. The locals are the first casualties . . . and never know how or why they got sick.

On a physical level, the micro-mist with microscopic droplets invades a far greater territory. Also, unseen and unmeasurable, the very disruptive metaphysical energy of glyphosate spreads over an even larger area, regardless of how the wind blows. As an energy of *dis-ease*, it permeates the people, the houses, their gardens and their lives. Its effect is slow and insidious as it slowly disrupts the human system. We give lip service to the physical, but it is the unseen and negative energies that can cause the greatest damage to us.

As a result of our unnatural alienation from Nature, our overall physical health is on a steady decline, with cancer and other life-killing diseases on a rapid increase. Despite the miracles offered by the skills of modern-day surgery, we depend far too heavily on the pharmaceutical drug companies that, like leeches, feed on human sickness. We pay a huge price for placing our health and wellbeing into the hands of Big Pharma. As, in our modern world, we become ever more isolated from Nature so it fosters the rapid breakdown of our mental and emotional wellbeing.

Enough . . . there are many books on these facets of human insanity!

Conversely . . . it need not be this way.

It is ironic when you realise that all creatures prosper by living in harmony with Nature. They are metaphysically connected in life and, when they go through the transition of so-called death, they *remain* consciously connected. This connection with all life on both a physical and metaphysical level is natural; we have mostly turned our backs on natural and live *largely* unnatural lives. It is interesting that the non-intellectual but inherent conscious intelligence of Nature knows and expresses itself as the consciousness of One. For most people Oneness is a vague concept, thought about by a few but very rarely experienced. It is one thing to intellectually know about the web of life, but it is something else altogether if you experience it. And *we can* experience it, *but not via the intellect.*

With the intellect viewing the world and life as outside of itself, it is natural enough that we have become onlookers of Nature, rarely participants. Very few people realise and/or experience life as an inside-of-Self process. We look through our eyes at the collective belief illusion of the world around us, and for us, that is life. This is where we can learn so much from Nature. Nature has almost the opposite experience of life. Nature is a total participant in life, never an onlooker.

Imagine a couple of left-brain dominant people walking through a forest. They are either both plugged in to their iPods, or they are in conversation, or both! They walk through the forest, yes, but they do not participate in the *experience* of forest. They are onlookers, looking out through the windows of their eyes at a forest that they perceive as outside of themselves. And from an intellectual viewpoint, they are correct; the forest they see *is* outside of their physical bodies. A convincing outside-of-self experience. They may name the birds, the species of trees, and maybe even the different species of lichen and liverworts on the trunks and limbs of trees, thus proving for themselves how much they know about Nature. In whatever way people experience or interact with a forest is up to them, but if it is left-brain oriented, it is an experience that is purely with a physical Nature.

Imagine now two people who are right-brain oriented. They are here to experience the forest, so they are silent. They walk slowly, maintaining as much inner quiet as is possible for them. Their mind-chatter slows down. They often stop to squat on their heels, still and quiet. Gradually they become more conscious . . . and they are listening. They hear many sounds, both close and distant, but they ignore this. They are listening to the silence.

Very gradually, as they slowly progress through the forest, the forest begins to interact with them. The energy of forest deepens within their inner awareness. If they remain silent, insights about forest life blossom within, revealing facts about which they previously knew nothing. They might feel a vast, yet nebulous presence growing within their awareness, yet they remain quiet. They feel deep inquiry, but they have no questions. They are beyond the place of questions, in the profound space of conscious experience. They feel a sense of Oneness, of resonant connection, but they allow the silence to be undisturbed.

And so it continues, as they are led ever deeper into the greater reality in which the secret Nature abides. This is not a forbidden zone; it is open to any human who has the humility to know their true place in the grand scheme of Nature. But this humility is not easily found, for while the intellect can mentally define it, it can never truly experience it.

Through the evolution of our many incarnations we have drifted into, and live in, a place of illusion — an illusion that relates only to a physical Nature. What we see is based in the human intellect, not in the reality of a metaphysical Nature. A case in point is competition. We see competition in Nature simply because *we* are competitors.

Most people compete in life. We compete against each other to the extent we have turned competition into professional sport. Not that there is anything wrong with this. But, we pay a price. Higher dimensional humans never compete with each other. Like Nature, they *cooperate* with each other. Even though we see our surrounding Nature as highly competitive, it is not as we see it. We see through the eyes of separation and competition, and this unreal view creates our misplaced intellectual view and misunderstanding of Nature.

A gardener with a green thumb is a person who loves growing

plants. This type of person is rarely competitive. I am one of them. As a boy I avoided competition, and I still do. I never *knowingly* compete. Types like us have a connection with Nature that is deeper than most, for we find Nature to be totally non-judgemental of us — a safe place. However, although we are comfortable with Nature, this does not necessarily mean that we are all comfortable with other people; many of us are not. For me, this was a learned process.

People intellectualise Nature, which is ridiculous because Nature is entirely non-intellectual. Why do we do this, believing the stories that our left-brain fabricates? Why do so many people become dependent on what our intellectual science offers? It is because the left-brain needs to understand. As I hope to reveal to you through these pages, the secret Nature is Mystery; Mystery to be *experienced*, never understood. But because the left-brain cannot embrace Mystery, it has no choice but to take a purely intellectual approach to an entirely non-intellectual Nature.

Nature is a **vast** diversity of expressions of conscious intelligence. From the functions of our left-brain, we classify and identify intelligence as a function of the brain. This logic is seriously flawed. I classify intelligence as the expression of an aware consciousness. The higher the consciousness, the greater the possible expressions of intelligence. By their very actions, this suggests that our world leaders and politicians are basically devoid of true *conscious* intelligence, hence their lies, corruption and hidden deceit.

Nature teaches in so many ways. As we all know, buds simply unfold to reveal their hidden flowers. People far too commonly stay as tight buds through all the years of their lives. Certainly a few manage to unfold their petals, slowly shedding the anger and judgements that have kept them shut down for so long . . . lifetimes! Some do let the blight of blame fall from the bud, allowing the winds of change to rip from the buds all the self-created detritus that has kept the buds closed . . . and they unfold. Most do not manage this. They hold tightly to their blame, their anger, judgements and their self-destructive habits. They hold tightly to their self-righteousness and pious pettiness, thus remaining as buds, hiding within the crushed and crippled flower of their negative beliefs. They never find the way to open the bud of their greater potential, the bud of greater possibilities.

The flowers in Nature simply unfold their petals and bloom. They never judge themselves as not good enough, or not beautiful enough . . . they never judge, period. They simply *allow* the rain and the sun to nourish their greatest potential, and they unfold into perfect flowers. In Nature, there are no better or worse flowers, just differences. And Nature is all about encouraging the expression of the uniqueness of differences. We tend to shy away from being different, wanting to conform, and yet such is our complexity that we often conform in our differences. We are inclined to fear other people's opinions of us, thus overlooking the self-damaging judgements that we are all too often heaping upon ourselves.

When it comes to comparing ourselves with Nature, we do not fare well. The left-brain view is that we are a superior creature, above and beyond the world of animals and other creatures. We live and judge from and through our intellects, never realising that the majority of people live the most superficial of lives. We believe in success and failure, tormenting ourselves with our stupid and erroneous, unserviceable beliefs. Success is to win, while failure is to be unworthy, feared.

Does the pebble at the base of a mountain look up to the summit with the thoughts, "I'm a failure. I haven't grown in ten thousand years. I hate myself."? The pebble is the pebble, the mountain is the mountain. As One they experience consciousness as One. Size is irrelevant. Separation, unknown.

How does one define Nature? This is a question that I have been asked. To me, Nature is the vast power of the evolution of Change on Earth. Nature is, literally, the consciousness of evolution through perpetual Change.

When I was a farmer, I became aware that I needed Nature to be on my side. Many farmers have made Nature their enemy. How stupid is this? They attempt to force the growth of pasture via chemical stimulation. To be fair, they call it fertilising — and probably believe it! Each year they apply the chemical stimulation, it forces the soil into unnatural action, just as a drug can as easily force us. As the years roll past, the living soil gradually becomes less alive, gradually losing the abundance of micro- and macro-organic life forms. The natural larder of the soil becomes ever more empty, ever more bare. Along with this, the natural chemical/mineral component of the soil gradually becomes more complex, forcing the soil into a retrograde cycle.

You could liken the soil to being the pantry of fertility. Each year fertility is taken out, and never put back. On hundreds of thousands of farms all over the world, the pantry is almost empty. The next step is GM, the genetic manipulation of sick, unnatural plants to produce sick, unnatural food in sick, degraded soil.

To our eyes, the GM vegetables look perfectly healthy on a physical level, but metaphysically their energy is completely unnatural, and seriously contrary to our health and wellbeing. This massive exploitation of our food happens when people lose their connection with Nature. If we were all connected, such food atrocities would never exist. If we were connected to Nature, people would realise that the bulk of our food is poor in quality. If we were connected to Nature, people would not want apples coated in wax to *look* nice. If we were connected to Nature, we would shy away from citrus that are sprayed with systemic poisons from the time of flower bud to the picked fruit. If we were connected to Nature, the energy of our food would tell us all we needed to know about it.

However, you *can* find this long-lost connection and resurrect it.

Summary: In this chapter I have attempted to establish that our alienation from Nature comes with a huge price tag. And unfortunately, though inevitably, more and more people are paying that price with their increasing sickness.

To communicate and truly connect with Nature requires that we once again reconnect with Nature on every level. Although I write of the physical and metaphysical Nature, they are One. I have met gardeners who would scoff at what I have written here, and yet they live it. Their connection with their gardens is vital to their wellbeing. I remember a particular show on the long ago television series, *Burke's Backyard*. Don was talking with a woman in her early eighties about being able to work in the garden at her age. She pointed across the garden. "You should go and chat with my mum." Don then went to the mother who was busily and happily weeding. She was 102! During their conversation she vigorously declared that it was her love of the garden and being in Nature that was keeping her fit and well.

Chapter Six

LOOKING AT . . . AND SEEING

Eventually, when I went down to the water's edge and looked at the river, I saw it as continual newness. I smiled in delight. It seemed so simple now. What was the difference? As I thought about it, I realised that it is normal to look through the eyes-brain, they connect. However, by persisting, I had gradually learned to also look through the eyes-heart connection, which has always metaphysically existed. It is not a by-pass of the automatic eyes-brain; it is an inclusion, a more holistic way of seeing. I also suspect that, although this was a discovery for me, it has probably been known among indigenous people of various countries for ages . . . and just as probably forgotten! This is why I urge you to learn to look at — and truly see. It will be of invaluable assistance in connecting with a hidden Nature.

If you are going to have a relationship with the secret world of Nature, you cannot do it blindfolded. You need to have your eyes wide open. You need to know just how far removed we are from Nature in our everyday relationship with life. You need to know that our most common thoughts are completely focused in illusion, and that the secret world of Nature cannot be found in illusion. You need to be aware that what you eat and drink will affect the way that you think, along with the expressions of your emotions . . . whether in anger or appreciation. You need to realise that what we call natural and organic is more a term for our growing, aware consciousness, than it is regarding the energy of all the food thus labelled. Some fruit and vegetable shops and even a few supermarkets have been known to place 'organic' labels on non-organic produce. I like to think that this is not common.

To be fair, there are probably more aware, conscious and devoted food growers today than there ever have been. Sure, I know that before the birth of our ruthless agricultural exploitation by chemical stimulants during the last hundred years or so, all food was so-called organic. I agree, and the soil was more alive and vibrant with energy. But that does not mean that all the farmers were conscious and aware . . . they were not. I happened to witness and remember the advent of chemical farming, and I knew the nature of many farmers of that time . . . even though I was young! They were as keen to exploit the soil for more production and profit as the chemical companies were keen to exploit *them!* And I do not write this in blame or judgement. My father was one of those farmers, and while he intrinsically knew that natural, ecological approaches were the best way to go, the lure of more money and the glib, glossy illustrated literature won him over. He was also lured by his keen intellect, for obviously, chemical so-called fertilisers and greater production was surely the way of the future. Goodbye farmyard manure!

When I wrote of there being more conscious and aware bio-organic growers of today than ever, this is exactly what I mean. As a metaphysician I see it in the energy-field of their produce, and in their own fields of energy. Although I would not describe my inner-seeing as infallible, like a muscle, the more I use it the more it grows and develops.

As I have stated, a deeper relationship with Nature means that we must consciously remove the blindfolds. It means that we look at . . . and see. Sounds simple, doesn't it? But on the contrary, most people look at but never truly see. People look at Nature through the eyes of their intellect; through the eyes of their beliefs; through the eyes of their education; through the eyes of their parents and teachers; through the eyes of their peer group; through the eyes of David Attenborough's brilliant videos; through the eyes of yesterday, last week — last month — last year — last decade — last lifetime — countless lifetimes. All the *past.*

But, how few people look at Nature through the eyes of the moment, of NOW, the eyes of immediacy?

Very few, indeed.

Let me share a story with you. When I was farming on the foothills of Mount Arthur in Tasmania, the island state of Australia, I acquired some forestry land that was considerably higher up in the hills. These high foothills were covered in a meandering forest of various Eucalyptus, all doing their best to hide and smother the gigantic rocks strewn on the steeper slopes. It was wild and very beautiful. It was also home to a pair of wedge-tailed eagles.

To keep this simple, I carved out a couple of hundred acres (eighty plus hectares) from the jungle of tall bracken and scrub that overran some of the relatively treeless areas. All trees were left intact. I picked up countless trailer-loads of rocks and wood, taking it off the land that I had cleared. I put in a *huge* amount of back-breaking work on that unforgiving land.

One day, with the soil now covered in struggling pasture, I was slashing the bracken that still attempted to make a take-over bid for the land. I was on a tractor, a whirling power-driven chain slasher spinning behind me. It roughly tore the bracken stems apart, rather than cleanly cut them, thus hastening the demise of the bracken as it bled sap from this mechanical onslaught.

At lunch time I stopped the tractor, and switching off the engine, I stepped down. The silence that remained was startling. Eating a sandwich, I was aware of the silence, and puzzled. In a wild Nature, silence is rare. A crow cawing in the distance, the breeze sighing through the leaves, various insects humming or buzzing . . . and so it continues. But no, all was silent. So silent, in fact, it began to affect me. I was aware of my thoughts slowing down, ever slower. Very strange!

I lay down on my back for a few minutes of rest, staring up into the sky.

About a hundred metres or so above me, a wedge-tailed eagle was slowly spiralling round and around, hardly a wingbeat or a feather moving. As I stared at it, watching its natural grace, a thought came very strongly. "Wow. I would love to fly like an eagle."

In that moment, thought deserted me, and with an inner twisting lurch, I was suddenly aware of looking down from eagle eyes into my own human eyes staring up. I almost lost it then, but an energy stabilised me. (It would be years before I learned that Pan had overseen the experience.) As I slowly spiralled around above my land, I could see my beef cows' tracks that went far into the surrounding unfenced forest. (I did not previously know about the tracks, and later I followed them.) I could see the whole farm laid out beneath me, and I was aware of having an intense clarity and depth of eyesight that far exceeded my human eyes.

I suddenly became aware that as an eagle, I was looking through the eyes of immediacy — of the immediate moment. I was looking and *seeing* through a frame of conscious awareness, with a crisp sharpness of vision beyond any previous experience. That moment revealed to me the human way of looking at, but never *truly* seeing.

As I became aware of this and accustomed to it, everything changed. I was now looking through metaphysical eyes, and what I saw shocked me. I saw my human self lying next to the silent tractor. In front of me was a vast, deep gulf stretching across my land . . . and on the other side was the forest: Nature. I saw my own separation from Nature, the human separation from Nature. In that moment I determined that I would cross that implacable Gulf of Separation; this I *had* to do, no matter how long it took.

As this realisation hit home, the eagle folded its wings and dropped a few metres, and with a physical jolt . . . I was back in my body consciousness.

At first there was elation, revelation, only to be chased away by the cold reasoning of massive, overwhelming self-doubt. Within twenty-four hours I went into complete denial . . . but I could never forget. The magic of the experience was buried too deeply inside to dislodge, even though I tried. That experience proved to be life-changing.

Just briefly, change came thick and fast after this, and within a few years I had sold the farm, and with my family — wife and four children — we travelled right around Australia. Nevertheless, I was firmly bound to my task: to cross the Gulf of Separation between Nature and humanity.

It took me fifteen years. I did cross the Gulf, only to find that it did not exist. A paradox: the Gulf of Separation is created by intellectual-mind, and intellectual-mind cannot cross it. I also crossed the equally non-existent gulf between physical-self and metaphysical-Self, but all this is another story for another time. Enough to tell of my gratitude to the eagle that showed me a glimpse of my potential, and the *truth* of my Being — and that of us all.

Despite the life-changing power of that experience, I was not gifted the ability to see through the eyes of immediacy — it would have been nice! I had to learn how to do that for myself.

The learning process is a story that is entirely relevant.

Back to my old teacher of early days . . . the river.

One day while I was learning to listen to the silent voice of the river, it asked me a question. *Do you see me as new?*

This was a seriously disconcerting question. If I stared at one spot on the surface of the water, then all the water looked exactly the same, every day. I could not see it as new. This disturbed me, as the ever-flowing water was obviously new in every moment, the most perfect example of life's continual renewal. Yet all I could see was more of the same water. If I stared at a small area of the same water, I would need to walk along the river bank to keep that same area in my sight. This also defeated me.

I struggled with this for a long time. I was busy practicing my listening skills which needed some improvement, like . . . did the river really ask if I could see it as new, or was that the mind playing tricks? *I knew*, but sadly, I also strongly doubted. Doubt and I were close companions! For months I practised looking at the river to see newness while listening to the river to be sure it was not laughing at me!

After nearly a year of this, my intent was still unwavering. In hindsight, I now know that when you set your *intent*, life will take you seriously. But, you are also required to persist. And persist I did. I spent most of my practice time in attempting to see the newness in my late wife, and my children. Month after month passed by, yet they remained aggravatingly the same. Same river, same wife, same kids, same me, same old same old. I was literally overwhelmed in sameness, but bereft of newness. I even wondered if what I was attempting was possible. But I kept on, feeling increasingly ridiculous.

One morning, just as I awakened, I heard/felt words moving through my consciousness. *Only the newness in you can see the newness in the river and in other people.* I thought it was the river speaking as it seemed to carry river energy. Later I confirmed this.

From this point I began to look for the newness in me! Phew! That took another six months or more, so we will skip over this, simply saying that there came a breathtaking moment when I discovered the newness in me. Then, from the foundation of this startling newness in me, I started looking for — and eventually *seeing* — the newness in my wife and children. I remember my initial excitement, and the frustration of being able to tell so few of my friends; but my late wife knew, and she understood.

Eventually, when I went down to the water's edge and looked at the river, I *experienced* it as continual newness. I smiled in delight. It seemed so simple now. What was the difference? As I thought about it, I realised that it is normal to look through the brain-eyes, they connect. However, by persisting I had gradually learned to also look through the heart-eyes connection, which has always metaphysically existed. It is not a by-pass of the automatic brain-eyes; it is an inclusion, a more holistic way of deeper seeing. I also suspect that although this was a discovery for me, it has probably been known among indigenous people of various nations for ages . . . and just as probably forgotten!

This is why I urge you to learn to look at . . . and *truly see*. It will be of invaluable assistance in connecting with a hidden Nature.

In modern people our eyes have become lazy. We wear glasses, not always because we truly need them, but because we accept lazy eyes as normal. I include myself in this. I wear glasses to read. We no longer need to hunt for our food, constantly scanning distances for food and/

or close by for danger. We no longer have our lives depending on our ability to see with the immediacy, clarity and intentness that such a situation demands. We no longer need to *see* the energy of a plant, instantly *knowing* whether it is a potential food, or a fast or slow poison.

Lazy eyes tend to see their surroundings as flat, without ever realising it. Landscape artists train themselves to see. When we look at a landscape painting done by a skilled artist, we marvel at the depth within the picture. Why is this? Because we seldom consciously focus on the true content of the scenery that surrounds us in daily life. Seen it before, know what it is . . . lazy eyes! A good artist has the ability to present a landscape to us in such a way that it almost seems to leap off the canvas — or draw us deep into the painting. We need our artists.

In the same way, the plants in the gardens of those of us who are blessed with gardens — many are not — almost unfailingly flower year after year. There are those who see the *same* flowers every year, and there are the fewer who see those flowers as totally *new* each year. The shapes and the colours are the same, but each year they are brand new and, in the garden of a garden lover, they have an ever-increasing energy.

Summary: We have now established that looking and *seeing* are very different. Obviously you are going to need to truly *see* the Nature that surrounds you if you plan on having a meaningful relationship with it.

If you travel around Australia you will drive across what is known as the Top End. This is the long, long stretch from the east coast across the top of Oz to the west coast on the other side. I have heard many people describe it as a very boring drive with nothing to see. This is a common description, but a hugely inaccurate one. What they really meant was that the long drive was short on entertainment. Of course, with our current electronic toys and movies those people can now do the drive without looking out the window, apart from the driver. And they get so bored they are prone to falling asleep at the wheel. I have driven across the Top End, and sure, it can be a constant low scrubby desert for several days, but if you get out and become a brief partic-ipant in that dry land you will find reptiles under the slabs of wood and old tree bark that abound, along with a surprising number of flowering plants. You will find plants that have adopted some very ingenious ways to make sure that you spread their seeds . . . and sometimes painful ones. My point is that it is a *living* Nature, not boring at all.

Get out in Nature. Look at it from new eyes . . . *and see newness.*

Chapter Seven

ON CONSCIOUS AND SUBCONSCIOUS

Most of humanity lives in a collective subconscious. The word sub basically means 'not conscious of'. So subconscious actually means 'not conscious of being conscious'! This, in turn, means that we operate as less than fully conscious. It is estimated that over ninety percent of the entire human population lives subconsciously. Even more scary are the people who believe that this is to our advantage; that we can train the subconscious to do the things that we do not consciously have time for. Sure, we can programme the subconscious to do many things, including making money, but the downfall is that, programme it as we may, we cannot programme it to subconsciously grow in consciousness. Today, most of humanity is an ever-repeating subconscious programme from our past as we continually repeat our own histories. This is the chain that anchors us to our ongoing self-destructive sameness. Truly, this is not a good path to walk! It is a path that can only eventually lead us into sickness and insanity.

What is Nature? Nature is the *natural* evolution of consciousness. What is humanity? Humanity is the *creative* evolution of consciousness. Both of these questions and answers apply only to life on planet Earth, in our particular part of the solar system. Even on our planet there is far, far more involved, but for now we will stay with just humanity and Nature.

So what is the actual difference between Nature and humanity? Now there's a question, for despite all being One in *consciousness*, the differences in *expression* are vast beyond comprehension. I cannot over emphasise this.

Nature is *permanently* fully conscious.

Humanity is *rarely* fully conscious.

Obviously this poses a bit of a problem. Actually, it is a huge problem if you have any intention of communicating with Nature or entering the secret world of Nature. How do you connect if you are forever subconsciously *outside* the moment, and Nature is forever consciously *inside* the moment?

Please be aware I am not making statements like this to put you off communicating and/or connecting with Nature. On the contrary, I want you to be very clear about what works for you regarding this connection and what does not. I am sharing a lifetime of my experience, learned on both a physical and deeper metaphysical level. I am also being fully honest with you about my personal experiences and how they will, or may, apply to you. I have no intention of offering you a few glib, but useless sugar-coated techniques that contain no depth of truth or honesty. What I am writing in this book has the capacity and the potential to transform your whole life. But of course, this rests with you. You will either add it to the intellectual library of your current knowledge and it will be wasted, or you can use it as a key of opportunity to open the door to something new, remarkable, and utterly exhilarating.

Let us briefly look at some of the various expressions of consciousness with which we are familiar. We have all read and heard about the great human unconscious. You hit me on the head with a heavy piece of wood and I am knocked unconscious. Right? No, actually this is false. What you have done by hitting me on the head is to disconnect my brain awareness from consciousness. Consciousness continues, but I am unable to connect with it because my brain has been temporarily stunned. We erroneously call this unconscious. Not only that, but we have had people like C G Jung who claimed that we all exist in a vast human collective unconscious. And as he taught this, other people knowing no better did not see the flaws, thus they accepted and believed this nonsensical teaching simply because they were not, and have seldom, if ever, been fully conscious. Finally, this teaching has become an established belief, a dogma, a so-called fact . . . all based in illusion. I find it scary that such a fallible fabrication can become credible.

Any person who is fully conscious would *experience and know* the falsity of this immediately. You cannot un-consciousness because this is not possible. Consciousness is the metaphysical awareness of what we call life. *Consciousness is life.* You cannot un-life, even though we play the game by believing in death. The life/death equation is something else that humanity does not seem to vaguely understand. First and foremost, all life is metaphysical. The metaphysical *precedes* the physical. If it makes it easier for you to understand, you could substitute the word spiritual for metaphysical; they are one and the same.

In reality, humanity is conscious. Many people who have been under anaesthesia for an operation — unconscious! — have detailed the whole long conversation between the surgeons who were operating on them. This has been well documented . . . yet somehow it is dismissed or ignored. Consciousness continues, whether the brain is anaesthetised or not, for we are able to function on other, higher, levels of consciousness.

The late, great J. Krishnamurti stated emphatically that there is no such thing as the unconscious. I just as emphatically claimed he was wrong, until I too eventually became spiritually enlightened. Smiling, I then metaphysically apologised to him. A statement from a master is often difficult for a student to comprehend.

However, what we *do have* is the collective subconscious. The word sub basically means *not conscious of.* So subconscious actually means not conscious of being conscious! This, in turn, means that we operate as less than fully conscious. It is estimated that over ninety percent of the entire human population lives subconsciously. Even more scary are the people who believe that this is to our advantage; that we can train the subconscious to do the things that we do not consciously have time for. Sure, we can programme the subconscious to do many things, including making money, but the downfall is that, program it as we may, we *cannot* programme it to subconsciously grow in consciousness. Today, most of humanity is an ever- repeating subconscious programme from our past as we continually repeat our own histories. This is the chain that anchors us to our ongoing self-destructive sameness. Truly, this is not a good path to walk! It is a path that can only eventually lead us into sickness and insanity.

The only way to grow in consciousness is *consciously.* That's it. How do we live as the creative evolution of consciousness if we are subconscious, less than being fully conscious? Simply, we cannot. And unfortunately, as an immortal species that incarnates over and over, we are compelled to live and experience all the negative repercussions of being less than fully conscious.

Enough of that . . . to explain the length and breadth and dimensions of this in the ongoing journey of the immortal souls that we are is not necessary.

Being conscious means being conscious of living in the moment. We are mostly unable to do this. Why? Because we think. And thinking takes us out of the moment. We cannot think our way into the moment, only out of it. Thoughts take us into the past, which does not exist or into the future, which does not exist. Okay, once again we need to go deeper. As physical people in linear time we have the past, present and the future. Problem is, we are also metaphysical Beings living in spherical time, where all time occupies the same moment. Just because we give ninety-nine percent of our focus to physical and linear does not make it more real. Unfortunately, such a focus creates the illusions we unwittingly believe to be truth.

All that is true and real is the eternal moment. Nothing in Nature thinks. Indeed, nothing in Nature is able to. As I have said, most people can hold their breath for longer than they can stop thinking. Added to this is the fact that an animal has a very different relationship with time. We experience the passing of linear time. We want our time to 'somehow' entertain or educate us in whatever way is meaningful to us as individuals. An animal does not have a relationship with linear time; its relationship is with the immediacy of the moment. It also has a relationship with the passing seasons, with its own growth and development, with procreation, with times of hunger or of plenty.

A leopard can sit/lie wide awake on a rock, unmoving for hours on end. It does not experience boredom; it is fully engaged in the moment. The tip of its tail is in constant movement, twitching almost ceaselessly, seldom still. Liken this to its radar, investigating everything in its vicinity. The energetic movement caused by the flight of a bird maybe fifty metres away is noted, the health and vitality of the bird all registers. A movement in distant trees releases a scent for the nostrils to explore, while the tip of the tail analyses the movements potential for food, or maybe to hide from danger. The leopard is always thus engaged in its immediate surroundings, fully involved yet without physically moving, a total participant. Far beyond vigilance, this leopard is One with its environment.

As I am writing, I can see from my study window a spangled drongo that has a woven nest hanging from a eucalyptus tree about ten metres above ground. She sits all day, still and quiet, just looking around. Is she bored, fed up, checking her smart phone for the latest gossip? She is simply with the moment, guarding her eggs and keeping them warm. Time has absolutely no meaning for her. No time is passing her by, for her relationship with life is utterly unlike ours. It is not better, or worse, neither more nor less . . . it simply Is. Yet to connect with Nature we need to connect with that Is-ness; not to understand or dissect it, but to consciously experience it. And with practice we can do this.

We humans also have the potential of super-consciousness. I do not mean like Superman, but like a fully conscious evolved person. Being fully conscious precedes being super-conscious. This comes to very few. This is a state of consciousness that is rare and refined. It comes when a person knows and experiences themselves as One with all humanity, all Nature, and with creation as One holistic energy of creative Love. It cannot be chased, or manipulated, nor are there genuine techniques that make this possible; it is held within the expansion and growth of human consciousness.

A super-conscious person makes no judgements; their thoughts are slow and deep and, at will, they experience periods of inner silence. They are aware that Love is the power of creation and, although they still experience the full power of emotions, they are no longer attached to them, nor to their outcome. They are also fully connected to the eternal soul they are, living a life of synchronicity.

Summary: We have established in this chapter that you cannot truly connect and communicate with Nature on a subconscious level. It is to your overall advantage to practice being aware and conscious in everyday life. You cannot separate connecting with Nature from connecting with people and with life. No matter how it may appear to be, energetically, nothing is separate. If you begin with a left-brain premise that you are separate and you have to *learn* to connect, you will fail. If anything, you will need to *unlearn* a lot of false beliefs. You begin your new conscious connection with the premise that you are already One with Nature. You build on a greater reality that *Is*, rather than attempt to construct a new reality based on intellectual illusion.

I recommend that you practice being aware of being conscious. Sounds strange — funny even — but it is the path to a greater relationship with life on all its many levels.

Chapter Eight

FEAR — PEOPLE AND NATURE

When an animal runs from another, we instantly relate to this as fear. From the animal's perspective this is not so. We think that it is in fear of losing its life, but an animal has no such thought, nor can it have. It knows itself as life. Death is not within an animals consciousness, nor was it inbuilt into us. It is we who put death into our consciousness! All animals have an inbuilt programme for survival. Why? Because every animal species is consciousness seeking to grow through the vast multiple diversity of the many species that exist. When an animal runs from a predator, its whole fight–flight–freeze programme/instinct kicks in. Why? Because the programme is designed so that every animal can experience the greatest possible extrapolation of the potential of the consciousness expressing in that animal form. Thus a rabbit runs from a fox. If it did not there would be no rabbits, and no extrapolation of their potential in consciousness.

We tend to think that fear is a single, basic energy that is presented to us through our many different experiences. To we humans there is truth in this, but there is more concerning the subject of fear than meets the eye. There are our own many human fears, and there is the fear we see and perceive in the natural world of Nature.

Not all is as it seems.

I strongly suspect that all my readers will be very familiar with fear. I suspect, equally strongly, that very few would actually be able to describe what fear truly is. We experience it but we seldom contemplate its energy, or the nature of it. To us, fear is a very common negative emotion.

55

In my Intensives I have occasionally referred to my earlier years when fear, literally, controlled my life — as it does for billions of people. I have jokingly said that if we each have a quota of fear, I had used mine up by the time I was forty-nine and three months. Now, I never experience fear. I choose Love, never fear. Most people have a reasonable fear of pain and sickness, and quite strongly fear the actual dying aspect of death. I *know* that death does not exist, so I do not fear it. The transition from physical to metaphysical — that which we call death — is as much a part of our personal creation as our whole physical life was! I definitely choose Love as the dominant energy for my eventual transition away from the physical.

When I listen to people talking about fear, I realise that most people speak words of ownership, as in *their* fears. Never claim fear as yours. This is not a good idea. Okay, certainly you created it, but you do not need to stake a claim on it!

Fear comes from our collective subconsciousness. The subconscious is rather like a metaphysical reservoir that is filled with our more meaningful experiences of the past . . . meaning many lifetimes of our linear past. The so-called *bad* experiences invariably left us feeling emotionally disturbed to varying degrees. One incarnation followed another, and over and over the disturbed emotions created ever more emotional disturbance; all this is on a sub-emotional level which, with along our subconscious thoughts, is the deep, unrealised content of our subconscious living. Those disturbed emotions also grew ever-increasing and disruptive fears. Now, in our modern times, through psychiatrists, psychologists and counsellors, we attempt to intellectually deal with our disturbed emotions/fears. Although this does have some measure of success, it is commonly more temporary than permanent. The clever intellect may well be able to understand the many expressions of our emotions, but ultimately, it can never experience them.

Unfortunately, the more violent the experiences, the longer they linger in our subconscious. Within this emotional/mental subconscious reservoir, our trauma and drama is by far the most powerful. Our terrifying experiences all have a strong, sometimes ferocious, impact on us, thereby creating very powerful imprints in the subconscious. Obviously all this trauma and drama is highlighted and imprinted with fear. Fear we cannot understand.

Although not in our easily accessible mental memory, these memories are deeply held in the timelessness of our emotional and cellular memories, and the memory of our psyche. When the familiar cue for fear is presented in our current life, so these old negative fears come surging out of the deep subconscious. Ask yourself, do you ever consciously choose fear? Do you ever think to yourself that you will now choose to be frightened? Seriously — never! Fear comes bubbling up in a single moment, overwhelming you, your thoughts and your current emotions as they are submerged in the darker fearful sub-emotions. All this comes from the past, *never from the moment.* Do you realise this? With no disrespect, most people are breathing, walking, living *reactions* waiting to happen. Fear always *reacts.* Love always responds. A reaction comes from the past, a response comes from the moment. Fear is a reaction. Love is a response.

Another aspect of human fear needs to be brought forward for you to be aware of. Human fear is based in our imagination. We tend to think that if we imagine something, it is not real. We align imagination with fantasy. This is a misconception. When you have some spare moments, Google for stories of people who have died from an *imagined belief*, not from their life being in any real or immediate danger. Let me be clear about this: they died not from any danger of death in their situation, but because they strongly *imagined* that their situation would kill them. There are many such stories, the following is just one of them.

Without going into details, there is a harmless non-venomous snake in Africa that appears as the exact image of a well-known highly venomous snake. This is the harmless snakes defence system. Quite a number of native Africans who have been bitten by it, have died. They imagined it to be the venomous snake, so the bite proved fatal. Their fear of the snake created their terminal imagination. And a highly fearful and negative imagination is definitely a terminal condition.

So what does this prove?

Okay, this gets serious. All human life takes place within the framework of certain universal principles. These principles are unwaveringly powerful. This is the principle that applies to imagination. *Consciousness does not know the difference between a powerfully imagined happening and an actual live, physical happening.* Why? Simply because, in consciousness, there *is* no difference. It is all timeless energy.

Most of humanity ignores these universal principles at a high cost. Once we live outside the boundaries of Truth, then we live in our own self-created illusions. And illusions kill. Among these, our misuse of imagination is probably a prime killer. I honestly think that most death certificates should have written on them: 'Death by misuse of the imagination'. Invariably, it would be accurate. As the Buddha said, "Every human being is the author of his own health or disease."

I am in no way attempting to prove anything in this *very brief* overview of human fear. I am attempting to steer you in a direction that most people do not go. You are *not stuck* with fear. It is not a contagion, and yet, paradoxically, it is contagious! Another triumph of human complexity. One person panics in a crowd situation and the panic spreads with devastating speed and results.

It need not be this way. You can free yourself from fears and experience the freedom that comes with this. Fear is not automatic unless you are! *If you live on automatic — subconscious — then you live at the mercy of illusion, and sadly, illusion has no mercy.*

The brief account I have written about the subconscious, sub-emotions and fear, is the way I *see* the energy moving on a metaphysical level. On this higher frequency level *all* our emotions are within a timeless realm. When our emotions are highly charged with fear — the most negative of emotions — they energetically look like a physical cyclone/hurricane, as malignant energies grow ever larger and more powerful, swirling round and around. And, they are just as destructive.

I am going to push you just one step further. Metaphysically, all time occupies the same moment . . . spherical time. The negative fears and anger of this, your present lifetime, are strongly affecting your past and your future. Equally, this in turn is strongly affecting and increasing the fears in your current lifetime. Consider the metaphor of a swirling cyclone of negative emotions. As it grows in size and power, so the negative emotions are swirling through multiple lifetimes *simultaneously* . . . and all unrealised by us in our linear addiction and our metaphysical ignorance.

In my Intensives I teach people how to achieve emotional balance. Even though I talk about this quite thoroughly, few realise the incredible value that emotional balance can achieve for them. Once again, the intellect is attempting to understand something that it can never experience. This overly dominant mental approach to life does *not* work in our favour.

Now, hopefully, you are ready for a different type of revelation.

Our experiences of fear do not exist in Nature.

We perceive Nature through the framework of our experiences, but this gives us an inaccurate and very distorted view. Nature lives consciously and, quite honestly, there is no such thing as conscious fear.

Does this sound controversial? Good, read on.

As a metaphysical traveller, I have experienced the energy of many animals. In other words, metaphysically I have been in their consciousness with them: in their bodies, experiencing what they experience. And never once have I experienced any animal feel fear as *we* understand and experience fear. I will explain this in detail, because this is very important if you plan to enter the secret world of Nature. Illusion is not part of the Nature kingdom, only of the human world. And illusion and erroneous beliefs will keep the door to the Nature's secret kingdom tightly closed.

Nothing in Nature has imagination. This is ours alone in the physical world of Earth. Knowingly or unknowingly, with our imagination we, each one of us, create the direction and the content of our lives. I could write a book on this, but enough . . . this is a book about entering the secret world of Nature.

Considering that rats probably outnumber us by thousands to every person, we are very fortunate that they have no imagination! The same could be said of cockroaches and ants, outnumbering us at probably billions to one. Rats are smart, very smart, but this smart is based in their level of conscious intelligence, not intellect or imagination. They have a fast learning ability and are incredibly adaptive, with imagination they would make a very formidable enemy. Need I say that most people are their own worst enemy?

People commonly project their fear beliefs onto animals. A feral cat runs away from people . . . instantly people assume that this is fear. It is not *human* fear. Truly wild feral cats are extremely vicious. So they are shot, poisoned and harassed. The cat connects deep stress and pain with people, thus its preservation instincts says run.

One of the most memorable metaphysical experiences I have had with fear was being within a snake. It was one of my classic learning experiences. I was within the body/consciousness of a puff adder in South Africa. All was quiet and peaceful, with the puff adder just lying in the sun on a well-used path. The snake was not even in an ambush position waiting for suitable prey; it was well-fed and sunning itself. No thoughts — none possible. Inner silence, but so incredibly powerfully in the moment. A *nowness in the moment* that humans so very rarely experience.

A woman came striding along. From the snakes perspective, the woman's energy was a swirling cyclone of confusion . . . whereas the snake lived in a world of utter clarity. The woman saw the snake/me. She stopped, almost frozen with fear, screaming, for she was so very close . . . well within the snakes striking distance. As the snakes tongue flickered in and out, quivering, I could easily taste the pheromones that were coming from the human. How do I describe this? The energy of the pheromones was like an abomination, something unnatural and utterly repugnant. It was like a smell/taste/touch of *anti*-life. Oddly, the flavour of fear held violence. I could feel the hostility in the snake rapidly gaining momentum. Its whole instinct was to bite and kill the abomination, the anti-life, that which does not exist in Nature.

From within the snake I was aware that it was not the woman it was focusing on biting, it was the abomination of the violent anti-life energy. Unfortunately, the woman was the source of all this. In the nick of time, screaming, she leapt backward, well out of range of the snake. I could still taste the violence, the abomination, but it was receding as the human put more distance between us.

This was not my first experience of knowing that human fear and animal fear are so unalike they are not even related, but it *was* the most powerful. I am serious when I say the situation would have been very different if the woman had *consciously* . . . chosen Love! The woman, now well out of range, continued screaming. Ridiculous! I left the snake's consciousness and as I happened to physically be there, I stepped forward and stroked the snake. The woman was more horrified than ever, her screaming rising in pitch. She obviously thought she was not only confronted by a deadly snake, but now a madman was on the scene!

The snake however, enjoyed being stroked by a calm energy. After a few minutes I picked it up and placed it in the bushes alongside the path it had been sunning on. I then apologised for human fear and reactions.

It will be obvious from this account that I am not afraid of snakes. This is not about bravado, it is simply that snakes do not invoke fear in me. They never have. Huge spiders, okay, I shudder a bit, but snakes, no. There was a time when this undoubtedly saved my life.

I was in my mid-thirties on my farm in Tasmania, down by the creek. It was early evening, and with a .22 rifle, I was there to shoot a rabbit or two for dinner. Seeing a rabbit, I knelt down on one knee to steady my aim. I was wearing very short work shorts — fashionable in those days! — and as I knelt I had the impression of movement literally beneath my descending body. I peered along the barrel through the sights at the rabbit about fifty metres away, and in the same moment became fully aware of a large tiger snake uncoiling from between my knees. I was in a completely helpless position. I could not aim the gun at the snake . . . and with a single bullet it would have been useless. With my two bare muscular thighs one on each side of the rising snake, I was beyond vulnerable. I sighed. Was it all about to end here? Despite this, I was not afraid. I like snakes. I knew that the tiger is a highly venomous and reasonably aggressive snake, and that a single bite on my bare thigh would most likely be end of game.

The tiger snake gradually reared higher and higher, effortlessly moving its head ever closer to my face. Needless to say, I did not move, not a twitch. As the snakes head came level with my eyes, just a hand-width away, its forked tongue flickering and quivering, its head flattened in the manner of a cobra, but not as much. The only thought I had was how incredibly beautiful it was. This was now seriously close up and personal!

We stared at each other for what seemed ages, but was probably half a minute. Then, very slowly the snake lowered its body down to the grass, its tongue constantly flickering. Finally, with no hurry, its head now the normal shape, it glided away from me . . . and I took a long, deep slow breath.

If I had emanated fear, the outcome would have been very different. And would you believe, after all that, there was not a rabbit to be seen!

Okay, a few paragraphs back I mentioned elaborating on what we falsely describe as animal fear. An animal has no relationship with death. We view our personal physical life as life itself, and when the body dies we describe this as the loss of life. This is false. Sure, it is the end of yet another physical body, but all *life is immortal,* eternal.

An animal has a keen sense of its metaphysical and physical life as One expression. Not a duality, but One. We are about ninety-nine percent focused on being physical, with less than one percent focus on our immortality, the metaphysical. We then project this into the animal world. Wrong, it is not like this. The animal world is not like we are. We are the ones who have alienated ourselves from life, not the animals. An animal does not relate to itself as purely physical in the way we do, its relationship with itself is naturally far more holistic. It has not learned and developed the false illusion of separation.

When an animal runs from another, we instantly relate to this as fear. From the animal's perspective this is not so. We think that it is in fear of losing its life, but an animal has no such thought, nor *can* it have. It *knows* itself as life. Death is not within an animals consciousness, nor was it inbuilt into us. It is we who put death into our personal consciousness! All animals have an inbuilt programme for survival. Why?

Because every animal species is consciousness seeking to grow through the vast multiple diversity of all the species that exist. When an animal runs from a predator, its whole fight-flight-freeze programme/instinct kicks in. Why? Because the programme is designed so that every animal can experience the greatest possible extrapolation of the potential of the consciousness of that animal form.

Thus a rabbit runs from a fox. If it did not there would be no rabbits, and no extrapolation of their potential in consciousness. This is nothing to do with a rabbit fearfully running from death in the jaws of a big bad fox. It is a rabbit following its programme of preservation to achieve as much of its potential as it can. In this way the rabbit potential grows — and rabbit consciousness grows. And so it is with all animals, each in their own unique expressions.

It may challenge you to release the beliefs to which you may have been attached. However, if you are open enough and you do persist, eventually you may enter the secret world of Nature. You will then learn and experience a greater natural truth than is ever humanly realised. I often feel sad when I hear animal lovers saying that animals are just like us. They are not like us . . . not vaguely. Such a statement indicates that this type of animal lover has no idea at all about what a human Being actually is, or what their latent potential is.

Animals are neither less nor more than we are. They are life forms sharing this planet with us. We are all the One consciousness, One energy. The levels of conscious expression and intelligence available to us vary with animals and with we humans. On average, because all animals live fully consciously, they use more of their available conscious intelligence than we do. The higher the animals development, the more intelligence they use. We, living subconsciously, are unable to use conscious intelligence. We long ago began developing and substituting our intellect, having now reached the stage where we actually believe that the intellect is a form of intelligence. Now, the more clever your intellect, the more intelligent you are judged to be. For me, the opposite is true. These are the people who are furthest away from using their conscious intelligence.

Just look at our environmental record. Consider our rape of the Earth and her resources, our plastic-filled oceans, our ruination of the great rain forests. Intelligence in action? I do not think so. This is justified by our foolish intellects. Just look at our world leaders. Intelligent? Sorry, they are all very clever . . . and clever unfailingly holds hands with stupid!

Summary: We have now established that humanity has a relationship with fear that we have always projected onto animals. Animals can get highly stressed and bewildered to the point of death. A confused animal shows all the symptoms we identify as fear, but this is not human fear. Our fear is based in negative imagination. An animal does not have this imagination. Even when an animal appears to be terrified, it is actually a very high level of overwhelming, and very often fatal, stress.

Of course, I cannot prove this and our cynical, sceptical world of today is attached to needing, requiring, demanding proof. However, I am aware that most readers of my books have moved beyond the need of scientific proof, trusting instead the instinct, intuition and dictates of their hearts. This is the path you need to adhere to. *Trust* in your own deep intuition, your own inner knowing. If and/or when you learn to enter the secret world of Nature, you will learn lessons beyond your imagination.

Chapter Nine

A GREATER REALITY

Pan: *It seems you did not know that each human lives within the borders and boundaries of their emotions. Thought can stray further, but human emotions are severely limited and restricted. If you are going to enter my world of Nature, this cannot be. Your emotions will keep you out, just as they keep most of humanity out. Some shamans learn how to step across this boundary, and some use drugs to assist them, but in both cases the borders remain. If I am to be your teacher, this will not do. These borders and boundaries must be cast aside until they no longer exist in your reality. They are not part of a greater reality. You cannot be contained and be free.*

Obviously, reality is far greater than our mere physical experience of it. When you consider just the tiny proportion of the overall visual and audial spectrum that we experience, then you must wonder about the other ninety-nine percent!

It begs the question: what is reality?

What indeed. If your experience of reality is greater than the reality your family and friends experience . . . then what? How do you deal with it? Many people are faced with this dilemma; you may be one of them. Is it okay if you are engaged in a dialogue with Nature that nobody else can hear? Can you accept this and be relaxed with it? If you are able see other life forms that have no real physical substance; are you alarmed and disturbed by this, or is it easy for you to accept? Just a few of the many questions. It is not unusual for sensitive children to be faced with this predicament. Unfortunately, all too often the parents convince the child that it is all down to imagination, so a great potential in the child is lost.

As I have previously indicated, I too struggled with this. It took me a long time to accept my own awareness of reality. I eventually learned that it was not my personal reality I was experiencing, it was an aspect of a far greater reality. I was the one who personalised it. I had one exceptional, rare moment when I shared the secret world of Nature with another person, and to be honest, I badly needed that experience. I was so challenged by my changing reality that I was feeling lost, lonely, and increasingly threatened.

It is easy to write of leaving behind the common consensus reality of the masses; it is another thing to have this inadvertently happen to you. Of course, this was the outcome of my earlier commitment to cross the Gulf of Separation, but I did not know that then. All I knew was that the world of normality was slowly fading while being replaced with *then*-incomprehensible newness.

That shared moment with a friend was very precious to me. I doubt he ever realised it, he may not even remember it, but I will never forget. We were both living in an intentional community at the time in the Upper Thora Valley in NSW. It was an exceptionally beautiful rain-forest valley, but our ex-dairy farm communal property had many acres of open pasture, scattered with majestic trees, and was bordered by a crystal clear river along one side, with the thick rainforest pushing in along the other sides. It was late evening, and I was walking up the hill away from the community homestead toward the amenities block. The sun was setting, and we were reaching into one of those mystical moments of twilight. Suddenly, I noticed something very strange.

It was a common practice in the old days of subtropical dairy farms to have a huge *Morton Bay* fig tree — *ficus* — very close to the area where the cows waited to be milked. Unlike a modest, modern herd of two hundred and fifty cows, in those days a decent herd would be around twenty-five cows. Nevertheless, this would create a wet boggy area — especially in the wet season — so the ficus was invaluable, as they drank in vast quantities of watery waste on a daily basis. It actually did work very well. We had converted the old dairy on this farm property into an office/studio.

The farmer-owner we bought the property from had given up milking a few years prior to selling, and he had placed a large salt/minerals block under the shade of the ficus tree for his beef cows to lick. They thrived on it, but unfortunately the farmer failed to realise that the toxic salt was seeping into the topsoil and saturating the subsoil, thus slowly killing the beautiful ficus. As a result, when we took over the farm we had a dying tree on our hands. We tried many ways to restore it, but we were too late to arrest the deep salt contamination from within the tree itself. As a result we had to cut all the dead and dying branches out of the tree, leaving just the dead trunk with a few thick branch bases. We had little choice about this as the *ficus* is a softwood tree, and the heavy branches fall easily when the tree is dead — and people who may be underneath would not appreciate this!

So . . . as I walked up the hill in the twilight, I was startled to see that the whole tree was standing, complete. Every branch was in place, every twig, all glowing with a soft, luminous light. Not a single leaf, just the complete previous network of branches. As I stared in awe, I noticed Terrance, a close friend, also just beginning to walk up the hill about twenty metres away from me. He too, was staring at the tree.

I called out. "Terrance, can you see the tree?"

He called back softly. "Yes, it's incredible. It's . . . complete."

Reaching me, we stood silently together, just witnessing the tree.

During the next few minutes the twilight quickly faded, becoming darker, and the ficus tree gradually faded back to the huge, ugly tree trunk.

Terrance and I stared at each other. "You really, actually did see that?" I asked.

He nodded, and went on to describe exactly what I had also seen.

I realised then just how badly I needed to share a view of the secret world that was becoming increasingly familiar to me. Did it help that he was a close friend? Yes, for me it did. I have no idea what allowed two people to share such a rare phenomenon, only gratitude. All I knew was that my reality was changing, and the closer I got to the Mystery of Nature, the fewer answers I had to my questions. Eventually, over many years, I learned the art of inquiry: to seek, but to not *need* answers. I recommend it as a far wiser path than questions. Questions contain you in the intellect, closing many doors that the intellect cannot understand. Inquiry is open, opening the doors to Mystery ever wider.

What does this have to do with entering a secret Nature, you might ask? Only everything. Read again the second chapter, on the structure of reality. This is a chapter to read and reread. To enter Nature's secret realm you need to learn that while you physically remain in your familiar daily bandwidth, you will also need to become conscious of, and metaphysically active, within the bandwidth of a higher frequency. In this way you will be *consciously* occupying two bandwidths simultaneously. You actually live this way all the time, but *not* consciously. You will learn that the metaphysical world of a higher frequency is not the same as the one your physical body occupies. And yet, of course, they also share similarities.

What is reality? In Truth, the immediate moment is reality. Nothing else. And this immediate moment is different for every person. Many people will share overlapping experiences and other similarities, but the little differences are there. This indicates that every person experiences their own reality. And it is so. But for a species as emotionally insecure and deeply unstable as our current humanity on this world in these times, all experiencing only their own reality, would result in pandemonium, mass insanity. This brings us to the world of illusion. This is a world created by humanity where we believe that we all participate in the same fundamental reality. And in the world of illusion, we do. We live in a consensual reality where we all appear to have a similar world view. When a person wanders too far from the world view of right or wrong, should or should not, good or bad, acceptable behaviour or unacceptable behaviour, etc., such people are labelled as antisocial, nonconformists, eccentrics, weirdos, and other such labels. Generally, if a few million believe something . . . it must be right; this is how consensus reality works. The numbers have it! This is the birthplace of our religions. If you have a thousand followers, you have a cult. If you have a million followers, you have a religion! However, I will pass right over our Godless religions with no further comment, other than to say they have no place in a greater reality.

A question I am asked: can you enter the secret world of Nature in a greater reality and also keep your own reality? This depends entirely on your openness. Generally, you can keep your personal world reality so long as it is not a fearful one. If it is, then this world is your prison for as many lifetimes as it takes you to pierce the illusion. If your personal reality is Love based and very open, then imagined fear is a comparatively minor aspect. In other words, you can have your personal world reality as long as it seamlessly dovetails into a greater world reality with no conflict whatsoever.

Many years ago when Pan first came into my life as my mentor, I was quite fearful. My past lives carried far too much pain and suffering for me to easily escape the clutches of fear. (If you are curious about my relationship with Pan, it is well documented in the trilogy *Through the Eyes of Love: Journeying with Pan*.) As a mentor, Pan had little sympathy for my fears. His technique seemed to reside in throwing me head first into the metaphysical situations that compelled me to face my fears. And I had many!

This is a story that I have often told. Unrealised by people, we are all contained within the borders and boundaries of our emotions. It is not our thoughts that truly contain us, it is the emotions that accompany those fearful thoughts . . . these are the 'real' bars of the prison. Pan had become my spirit mentor, and despite my gratitude, I was struggling with the reality of this. It did not fit into my limited and conservative way of thinking.

One morning while still living in the Bellingen Valley, but no longer living in the community, I began to negotiate the steep bank down to the beautiful Bellinger River. We were living in an old house on the bank of this average sized river, perched well above it, out of reach of the regular flood waters.

The bank was very steep and I had hacked a series of crude steps into it. As I descended my rather steep steps, I could see the river through a gap in the undergrowth. This is where I had my old, often mentioned, bridge- board. (*Talking with Nature*). To my shock I could see Pan leaping up and down on my springing, super-flexible bridge-board with superlative ease. Part of my shock lay in the fact that the bridge board was about fifty centimetres wide and about ten centimetres thick, and was about as flexible as an average brick!

Yet here was a very physical-looking Pan making it very flexible. This was not even remotely possible! When you get a shock of this nature, your brain goes blank. It cannot process what it sees because what it is seeing is utterly impossible! I was so blank and shocked that my brain decided I must be dreaming. Still blank, I reacted by smacking myself around the side of my head so unintentionally hard that I knocked myself off my feet, crashing to the ground. I hurt! Okay . . . this was no dream; I was awake and Pan was still leaping. I shakily proceeded very carefully down the rest of the steps. I tried not to look at Pan, but it seemed that I could not look away. His energy held my eyes relentlessly as I continued downward.

When I stepped onto the river bank, Pan was directly before me. My old bridge-board was securely wedged in its usual position, and Pan was doing the impossible.

Gazing directly into my eyes, Pan leaped high, his landing forcing the bridge board to powerfully flex. It threw him even higher into the air where, totally impossibly, he spun into three slow, incredibly graceful somersaults. He then paused in the air for long moments, only to finally land feet first lightly on the surface of the river, without so much as hint of a splash.

He stood on the water's surface staring at me, his expression filled with compassion. He knew exactly what I was going through.

This might sound like no big deal, but the effect on me was unexpected and completely devastating. I fell to the ground, curling into a tight foetal position. I wanted to cry and cry and cry forever. I did shed copious tears. The borders and boundaries of my emotions had been shredded. What I saw was not in any way possible, but I watched it happen. No explanation would help, none was offered.

It seems you did not know that each human lives within the borders and boundaries of their emotions. Thoughts can stray further, but human emotions are severely limited and restricted. If you are going to enter my world of Nature, this cannot be. Your emotions will keep you out, just as they keep most of humanity out. Some shamans learn how to step across this boundary, and some use drugs to assist them, but in both cases the borders remain. If I am to be your teacher, this will not do. These borders and boundaries must be cast aside until they no longer exist in your reality. They are not part of a greater reality. You cannot be contained and be free.

All this flowed into me, as Pan continued my first real lesson. I know enough now to realise that in those shocking moments a greater reality and my personal reality came into juxtaposition, and that Pan was the architect of this shattering, painful, yet magnificent moment.

I remained curled in a foetal position, tears dripping from my cheeks. I find it impossible to adequately describe the fears that were revealed, or the shame I felt over these fears. I wanted to scream and scream my anguish as my rational emotions fought a losing battle with the revelation of a greater reality. I had my first lesson that our perceived impossibilities have no place in a greater reality . . . a lesson in letting go. In hindsight I often thought that it had been a rather brutal lesson, but as I reflected on my own nature, I long ago realised that nothing less would have been as efficient. It was not the end of such abrupt and shattering treatment, but nothing else came close to that first overwhelming experience as my emotions were torn away from their placid and familiar comfort zones.

Over time, those borders and boundaries were released, and I was able to experience a far greater freedom. If you are a very wealthy person in a prison, your wealth can probably buy you many adult toys to distract you . . . but you remain in prison. This is the conventional way of life. We do not see the borders and boundaries that hold us imprisoned,

71

even though we may often feel that something is missing. In vain, we attempt to fill that emptiness with the toys of wealth.

When you spend your whole life contained by our so-called physical laws you tend to believe in them. Defying gravity has severe repercussions. Once you learn this as a kid by falling out of a high tree while collecting rooks' eggs, you become a believer. And this means an emotional believer! Yet none of these fear emotions belong in a greater reality. They hold the fearful on a lower level of energy, making it almost impossible to enter into higher realms.

I have shared this story with you to illustrate my point. In this book I am offering you a way into another world. Never for one moment think that the greater reality of the metaphysical world of Nature is just a natural part of your physical world . . . it is not. Most of your physical reality is based in illusion, it is not truly real. It is a shared dream that we collectively experience. It is, and will remain, the basis of our physical world reality, and this is okay. But living that illusion for thousands of lifetimes with never a glimpse of something greater is truly unworkable. As immortal Beings we have forever, but who truly wants to spend forever in a dream that all too often becomes a living nightmare.

I smile as I remember a car oil TV commercial of long ago. A thug was telling the nefarious members of his gang about the virtue of 'good' oil in their getaway car, "Oils 'ain't just oils!" he said in a gruff, gravelly voice.

Equally, 'reality 'ain't just reality'. There are as many realities as there are people. We have our personal reality, a consensus reality, an overall national reality, and a wider basic global reality. These are all very well documented and acceptable because everyone is aware of them. Seldom do you find accounts of people's experiences in a greater reality, yet they are out there. Generally they come under a heading like strange phenomenon, or spirituality, or the twilight zone, or some such label of ignorance. This allows so-called normal people to avoid reading it, as many of them do *not* want their normality disturbed. Even though you are one of millions of exceptions — nevertheless, this makes you one of the few!

Before I leave this subject, just consider this. All your reality of today is based in your personal memories of the past. We all share many similar memories, similar stories, some horrific, others wonderful, but nobody *fully* shares their own personal mental and emotional experiences. It is from these that you create your daily life. Fear reacts, Love responds. This suggests that you, today, are a living reaction *or* response to your memories. You are either living a reactionary life based on your many negative memories, and you are struggling, or you are living a responsive life based on your many positive memories, and you are truly enjoying life.

All this . . . and the only reality is the reality of the unfolding moment. Imagine if you lived consciously in the moment without any undue influence from the past. This, dear reader, is the world of a free animal. Not a caged or pet or food animal, but animals that roam wild and free.

In the secret world of Nature, the metaphysical explorer enters a very different reality, leaving as much of their daily mental and emotional baggage behind as is possible.

Summary: We have now reached an understanding of why so few people actually enter the secret world of Nature. Far more people can communicate with the animals and trees and rocks and rivers of Nature than can actually *enter* their realm. Certainly these people gain an ever-deepening insight into Nature, moving well beyond the confines of our intellectual knowledge of the world of a physical Nature.

What I would like to establish is that for you to enter this secret kingdom you are going to need far more than the sum of wise words on how to do this. Personally, I never encountered any 'how to' books during my progression. I do remember being inspired by J. Allen Boon's *Kinship With All Life,* and there were a few others, but there was nothing telling me how to open that elusive door, or what to expect if I did. Like Frank Sinatra, I did it my way!

There are many pitfalls; this is why I am writing this book for you. I had to find my way, stumbling from one misconception to another, but never giving up. It was a path full of roads blocks (pun intended!). Obviously, my relationship with a mystical Nature is incredibly precious to me. The eventual, inevitable death of my physical body will only be a deepening of that relationship.

Chapter Ten

CONNECTION AND SEPARATION

You look at a forest as you walk among the physical trees and all the abundant vegetation — so this is a forest. This is rather like looking in a mirror at a reflection of yourself — so this is you.

Is it really? If you look into a mirror, you know perfectly well that the reflection in the mirror is not truly you; it is no more than a reflection of you. If the mirror is removed while you are looking into it, you know that you are not dead or extinct simply because there is no longer a reflection of your physical body for you to look at.

In a similar way, the material world of Nature is no more than the physical reflection in an unrealised mirror of a greater meta-physical Nature. Equally, if you remove the physical reflection from the mirror, this in no way indicates that the greater meta-physical reality no longer exists, or is now extinct.

When we look at the world through our physical eyes, we see a world of separation. Naturally enough, we believe it is as we see it. However, with only one percent of the electromagnetic visible spectrum available to us, this suggests that there is far more than we can physically see! Note that I write *physically* see. We have a metaphysical vision that works on a much higher frequency/bandwidth, but this is different from seeing through our physical eyes.

It is now a widely accepted philosophy that all living creatures are connected within a vast global — or even universal — web of life. Considering that everything is *One* energy, it becomes evident that One energy connects all life as One. It seems to have taken our physicists a long time to discover this, whereas it has been known for centuries by metaphysical practitioners.

A few years ago I listened to a physicist speaking at a conference in which I was also a speaker. It rather thrilled me when he detailed certain aspects of quantum physics that I have often seen in my metaphysical journeys. My pleasure was not about validation — I don't need it — but the fact that physics is inevitably moving in the same direction as metaphysics. One day they will meet on equal terms. For many years, during my metaphysical journeys in both Nature and the world of humanity, I have seen the torus — thousands of them — but I had not the vaguest idea of what it was that I was seeing. You can imagine my delight when watching the *Thrive* documentary/movie, to see a three-dimensional graphic image of a torus and to hear it named. I have seen many more different versions of them than seem to be currently documented. It is unquestionably a person's state of consciousness that determines the energy and expression of their torus. The human torus can range from being energetically beautiful to being very disturbed and malformed.

When we go for a walk in the forest we see all the separate trees that surround us. Physically, this is so. What we do not see is the connective web of life that pertains only to this forest . . . even if *intellectually* we know that it is there! The forest is a complex energy of One, expressing in what we see as a multiplicity of thousands of different plants that are all apparently separate. The paradox is that while physically they are separate, metaphysically they are all, energetically, One. Nature knows only Oneness and connection. Separation has no reality in Nature.

You look at a forest as you walk among the physical trees and all the abundant vegetation — so this is a forest. This is rather like looking in a mirror at a reflection of yourself — so this is you. Is it really? If you look into a mirror, you know perfectly well that the reflection in the mirror is not truly you; it is no more than a *reflection* of you. If the mirror is removed while you are looking into it, you know that you are not dead or extinct simply because there is no longer a reflection of your physical body for you to look at.

In a similar way, the material world of Nature is no more than the physical reflection in an unrealised mirror of a greater metaphysical Nature. Equally, if you remove the physical reflection from the mirror, this in no way indicates that the metaphysical reality no longer exists, or is now extinct. Most humans believe that we are more than a physical body. This suggests that we have a spiritual life, maybe even suggesting that we have a metaphysical (beyond the physical) body which is not visible in mirrors, or to other people when we are so-called 'dead'.

In the secret world of Nature, each tree that we see in a forest is the physical reflection of a greater metaphysical forest that we cannot see. Ergo . . . if we cannot see it, it does not exist. Wrong. It *does exist* on a different bandwidth. We, living on *our* bandwidth, do our best to define the world. This is rather like looking at a planet through a telescope that is fixed on a single tiny location and, from this fixed point, to then define the planet. Just as we limit ourselves to a definition of our world from a single bandwidth, so the telescope will carry our woeful limitations with it. From the one fixed location, the telescope would completely fail to see life if it existed on another continent, or on a higher than three-dimensional level. Hopefully, we would have the sense to acknowledge that we could not see enough of the planet to reach any sweeping conclusions about it.

We have exactly the same problem in our forest on Earth!

We *think* we can see all of the forest, and that it is *only* physical. Thus we shortchange ourselves from the potential of what could be a very different and illuminating forest/life experience. And the fun part is: if you were to experience the secret realm of the forest and write about it, only those who have a deeper connection with Nature would find it acceptable. Science would be more inclined to dismiss you with a couple of words: prove it. And you could not! You would need to make your peace in a world of humanity that unknowingly and subconsciously chooses not to *see* beyond its beliefs and accepted limits.

In my public talks, I sometimes ask the participants to look around the room at other people. We all appear to be separate. Yet, energetically we are One human energy expressing in separate bodies. We see only the bodies, we do not see the energy. A body dies, but the energy continues. This person now continues their unending life for a timeless period as a metaphysical Being, until they physically incarnate again. They will then once again continue both physically *and* metaphysically, all without being aware of their metaphysical reality. This is called normal. In this way we drastically reduce our holistic potential. In effect, most people live considerably less than a half life for as long as their physical body lives. Today, the Western World is so oriented on the physical that the death of the body is called a *life lost*.

How frighteningly ignorant: such an illusion does not serve us. You cannot lose your life; you *are* life. Bodies — which you are not — you *can* lose. You have already lost thousands of them, yet here you are reading these words in your current body. This is what happens when we live our lives locked in the belief of separation. We become part of a collective illusion which we then attempt to understand. And when we think that we do understand, we deceive ourselves simply because it is all just an illusion, but we don't know that and so the intellectual pain game goes on and on. You understand?!

Let me put a simple question to you.

We live in a world of fear, anger, blame, violence, mass poverty, deep-seated hopelessness and despair. We live with rampant sicknesses, with mental diseases, with anxiety and depression, and with ever-escalating suicides. Does this seem to be the result of Oneness and a deep inner connection with all life? Or is it possibly the outcome of all the endless fears that accompany our isolation and separation — our tragic disconnectedness? Of course, I should balance this by saying that the world is also full of Love and joy, of kindness and compassion, and life is likewise uplifting and fulfilling. But this is true only for the very few, and it has nothing to do with money. Money can buy almost anything except true freedom, peace, joy and happiness, or the experience of unconditional Love. No, this is experienced by those few who live *consciously* connected.

Okay, having made you more familiar with the various features of separation and connection and how this affects human life, we will look at this important aspect of life from the viewpoint of Nature.

I wrote of the *web* of life. I also mentioned how this is now becoming widely accepted. But how many of those people who understand the *concept* of a web of connection actually *experience* it? The problem is that although the intellect can understand a web of life *theory*, it can never experience it *in practice*. And this web of connection is not a theory, nor a concept, nor an idea . . . it is a reality that has always existed. While it remains only as an acceptable and intellectual hypothesis, some people will speak and write clever words about it, but they will always be words that are energetically empty of the real experience.

I have read of how the movements of a herd of bison in North America affect the movements of a mob of kangaroos in Australia — and vice versa. Very clever, but to me the writer had never experienced the herd of bison or the mob of kangaroos; it was a theoretical sup-position. Paradoxically, while I metaphysically experienced a herd of bison in Montana a few years ago, after over fifty years in Australia I have never consciously experienced a mob of kangaroos. It is still on my 'to do' list!

I first encountered this connection between animals and humans by way of a painful encounter with a herd of cows. This was the time when I first realised that my cow herd was more attuned to my personal energy than any of my human friends. The cows *energetically* knew me.

When, in my mid-twenties, I emigrated from England to Tasmania, the Island State of Australia, I became a beef farmer. A series of unfortunate circumstances within Nature that were far beyond my control, casually wiped out most of my beef cattle within the first eighteen months. It was a grim beginning to a new career. For economic viability I was compelled to become a dairy farmer. An undisciplined young man, it took me just eight weeks to learn that I hated the twice daily routine of milking cows. Self-discipline with a vengeance! Add to the milking routine the twice daily feeding of a couple of hundred pigs and bucket rearing a hundred calves; it was literally endless work. My day began at 5:00 a.m. and continued until around 7:00 p.m. Of course, during calving season, hay time and pasture work you could often add another couple of hours to my working day. On the positive side, at that youthful age I had a huge reservoir of energy. In point of fact, I am blessed to this day with a similar reserve of energy.

Back then, the state-of-the-art milking machines that are available today were non-existent. To be clear, I liked the cows, but milking . . . ugh!

Enough . . . the scene is set.

Not to my credit, I was mostly in an ugly mood when milking the cows, and they knew it. I had no idea *how they knew*, but they clearly did. The worse my mood, the more the jet-propelled, green, liquid shit flew from the cows, splattering over everything, me included. I have to admit, this did nothing to improve my mood!

This mayhem continued for about three years, when it all came to a rather violent ending. One of the long-legged cows kicked me as she came into the milking bail. She caught me on the big quadricep thigh muscle, nearly paralysing my leg. Sadly, for an Aries man who really did not have much of a temper, I lost it big time. I grabbed a leg chain, and swung it around my head intending to hit her hard across the ribs. (Yes, I know, disgusting! I was not always the beautiful man I am today — I had to grow him!) In my angry haste, I made the mistake of not securing her in the milking bail. As I swung the chain to hit her, she danced sideways and kicked out again at my aggressive and angry energy. The chain caught on her hoof, violently tearing it out of my wet hands. I doubt she even felt it. Now, the chain was whirling in a rapidly accelerating arc as it came hurtling back toward me . . . to wrap, in a blaze of agony, around my left arm. I almost fainted.

In that shocking moment of agony, I instantly and powerfully *knew* that I was the author of my pain and of all the dairy bedlam and turmoil. Why this sudden revelation should be so violently and traumatically thrust into my consciousness on a cresting wave of pain, I had no idea . . . but I knew and instantly accepted it.

I was laid up for several days. It took four months for the pain to leave the bone, the bruising was so severe. But it changed me. Only my wife knew that I had changed; she lived with me. None of my friends ever made a single comment about change in me. To them, I was the same old same old.

However, every cow in the whole herd of one hundred cows knew that I was changed. When I began milking again, all the cows were calm and easy. No green shit flying. No kicking. No jittery cows. I had never experienced it like this. I, also, was calm, finally accepting my situation with a fair degree of grace. And so it remained over the years for as long as I continued milking.

In those days I knew nothing of Oneness. Nothing of connection, but my cows certainly did. They lived it. They knew my field of energy better than I did. When my energy changed from violent to benign, they responded in a like manner. Over the following years, I explored what had happened. I now know that it was the beginning, and the opening, of my deep metaphysical connection with all life. That kicking cow gave me a precious gift, because nothing less than that level of violence would have broken through my shell of apathy. The shocking pain lanced an old abscess of smouldering intolerance that had finally reached its use-by date. And what perfect timing!

Summary: It is really important for you to accept that we live in two hugely different worlds, and that they both occupy exactly the same space/moment. This, in fact, happens on many levels, but the level to which I am referring is the World of infinite Holistic Connection and the more familiar World of Isolation and Separation. Ask yourself; which is the world that most holds your focus and your attention?

There is no right or wrong to this, no reprimand or criticism. I lived in the world of separation for many years, even though in my youth I often made field trips into the world of connection. For me, crossing the self-created Gulf of Separation actually revealed the World of Connection. For a person living connected with both worlds, the Gulf of Separation has no power over them.

This is how I live today. I am thoroughly familiar with the World

of Separation, but I am now a resident in the World of Holistic Connection. Do not get the idea that it has to be one world or the other.
Remember however, it is to where and to what you give your *focus* and
attention that your energy will flow . . . and connect . . . and empower.

Chapter Eleven

OUR NATURAL LIGHTNESS OF BEING

Where you focus your energy flows, and connects and creates. The normal human focus is erratic and unstable; all over the place. It is rather like a mayfly dancing over the water of a pond; lifting and falling in meaningless swoops, and very short lived. With practise, you are able to develop a steady focus. A simple practise is to sit in a garden or park and focus on any tree that engages your attention. I suggest a tree simply because the tree will assist you. All you need do is focus on the tree. You need not struggle with thoughts or attempt to stop them, but do restrain them from scattering all over the place. Focused is the opposite of scattered. If you must think — you will — keep your thoughts with the tree as your focus.

We are all very familiar with our physical bodies. We may not know — or care — about how they work or what is best for them, but we are constantly reminded that our physical bodies exist. Generally, when we are negligent with our bodies they tend to get sick and enfeebled, such as when we consume or imbibe low energy food and drink. Happily the reverse is also true, and bodies well into their eighties and nineties can be hale and hearty if their needs of nourishing food and healthy exercise are catered for. Sadly, this is too seldom the case.

You, dear reader, may be well aware that the physical body is a vehicle for the soul that you truly are. It is probably one of the reasons you read this type of book! However, as a generalisation, this is something that is seldom considered, nor is it commonly thought about. Yet it is this deeper aspect of self that I wish to now address. I have very carefully — even if briefly — described how Nature is fundamentally a non-physical expression of life. On our bandwidth we see a physical world reality, but move onto a higher frequency bandwidth and we see a greater reality. Obviously, just as Nature occupies both a physical and metaphysical bandwidth simultaneously, so the same truth applies to us. This is one aspect of duality.

You have a physical body and a metaphysical body. You will quickly realise that you have a ninety-eight percent of the time relationship with your physical body and the physical world, and about a two percent of the time relationship with your spiritual/metaphysical body and the metaphysical world. I am being extremely generous with the 2%! Whereas you can and probably do have a physical relationship with a physical Nature, this is just a snowflake on the tip of the proverbial iceberg with regards to your potential metaphysical relationship.

This book is about *entering* the secret world of Nature. My whole intent is to make that secret world available to you. Yes, it will entail a sharp learning curve and a fair degree of self-applied discipline, but should you succeed in your mission, you will have this new skill and ability forever. And forever is a *very* long time! Why forever? Because you will have grown in consciousness, and when a skill becomes an aspect of your consciousness, it is with you in every incarnation. In other words, you cannot enter this secret world and remain the same . . . any more than you can remain the same and enter this secret world!

We have a single physical body in each incarnation. It is enough! However, we have multiple metaphysical bodies all occupying the same space/moment with the physical, although they are on a higher frequency bandwidth. The several levels of emotional and mental bodies are not really relevant to this book, other than to say that you would be wise to develop and retain as much emotional and mental balance as possible. Nothing faked or forced, just a calm emotional and mental serenity.

When we do our 5-day Intensives, I have an inner exercise where I have people moving into a metaphysical situation which reveals to them their metaphysical body/self. It can be a very emotive experience to observe your own Lightness of Being for the first time.

If you have read any of my more recent books — they go back over forty years — you will be familiar with the term: *Light-body*. We all have this Light-body, but very few people are consciously aware of it. The common belief today is that we are physical only. A pity, because we are so short-changed with this *self-limiting* belief. To be honest *you* are a magnificent, metaphysical, multidimensional, immortal Being of Love and Light. Remember? And seriously, if you were to *live* this Truth in your everyday life, that Truth *would* set you free. Simple, maybe, but not easy! That old, old, long established belief that we are just a body has reduced us to the point where long ago the body became our prison. And yet, every night while sleeping we leave the prison as our astral body soars free — and we have our astral experiences, some of which we recall as dreams — only to immediately re-establish the prison status on waking up. Seriously, this is not a good idea. If you follow the opportunity I offer in this book, you can forever be free to leave that prison — but note, this does not mean 'dying'!

Where you focus your energy flows, and connects and creates. The normal human focus is erratic, unstable, all over the place. It is rather like a mayfly dancing over the water of a pond: lifting and falling in meaningless swoops, and very short lived. With practice, you are able to develop a steady focus. A simple practice is to sit in a garden or park and focus on any tree that engages your attention. I suggest a tree simply because the tree will assist you. All you need do is focus on the tree. You need not struggle with thoughts or attempt to stop them, but do restrain them from scattering all over the place. Focused is the opposite of scattered. If you must think — and you will — keep your thoughts with the tree as your focus.

You must not *try* to do this, you just *do* it. As soon as you *try* to do any of these practices that I suggest, you are using the left-brain, and it will not work for you. Your right-brain can do this simply and easily without trying. There is no time schedule for this; it is your decision. If you choose to avoid it, the experience I offer will avoid you. The allotted time that works best is when you go to the very cutting edge of your comfort zone. Eventually you find it becoming much easier. If you stay well within your comfort zone you will accomplish little. This applies to almost anything in life. Not fair, is it?

Okay . . . when you have developed an ability to hold your focus for a satisfactory time, you switch from the tree which you can physically see, to your own metaphysical Light-body which you cannot see physically. This is why you need focus. The tree will continue to assist you, for after you have spent so much focused time with the same tree, you are now connected in consciousness. How about that! You have made your first conscious connection with the inner world of Nature without even realising it!

Again, this Light-body focus will take you for as long as required by your current state of consciousness. You now know that as you consciously practice you are growing in consciousness. Interestingly, you could practice archery, for example, until you became an expert, but this does not mean that you will have grown in consciousness. You grow in consciousness when your *consciousness is fully engaged* in whatever the spiritual practice is. However, I will say that you could take your spirituality into archery, thus fully enriching the experience and consequently growing in consciousness. Nothing is excluded from your spirituality unless *you* exclude it . . . and most people unwittingly do this most of the time.

Let me be clear. You simply focus toward your imagined Light-body.

Imagine yourself as a body of Light which is about three times bigger than your physical body . . . and glowing with Light. You can have a shapeless Light-body if this works for you — but I do not recommend it. We are very familiar with our physical body shape and I always stay with this.

You are *not attempting to create it,* for this Light-body is always with you. Nor are you struggling to see it; you are getting to know it, to sensitise yourself into feeling it, into an awareness of it, an ever-deepening familiarity with it. And this all happens at your own pace and cadence. It is a bit like the old adage in England: How long will it take for my train to reach London? It depends on which station you get on the train. From Cambridge, not long. From Edinburgh, quite a while. This is how it is. According to the calibre and intent of our conscious spirituality, we are either closer or further away. But, the good news is that, as you consciously practice, you will be growing closer every time.

I am sorry that I cannot offer you a quick fix, a few easy gimmicks. Did I write that? No, I am not sorry at all. I honour *you* by offering you a *true way* into the splendour of the secret world of Nature. And *I* am honoured to do this.

Gradually, with practice, you will be using focus to grow and develop the Light-body which has for so long been overlooked and neglected. Remember, where you focus your energy flows, and connects, and develops. You are a creator and this is your birthright. One day, further down the track, you may perhaps become aware of the magnitude of that which you have created.

The day will come when you are ready for more. Ready to take your first metaphysical steps into a greater reality: the secret world of Nature. To do this it is wise to take assisted passage. Interestingly, the colours of the rainbow align with the colours of the chakras in our metaphysical body. I suggest that you consciously imagine, and if possible visualise, walking through the colours of the rainbow. Do this slowly, with no hurry or haste. Begin with red — base chakra — breathing and seeing and feeling red. Continue to orange — sacral chakra — fully experiencing orange. Next is yellow — solar plexus chakra — fully experiencing yellow, and on to green — heart chakra — fully experiencing green. On to blue — throat chakra — fully experiencing blue. Next is indigo — brow chakra — deeply experiencing indigo. You now move on to violet — crown chakra — immersing yourself in violet.

As you *consciously* go through these colours, so your frequency rises with the increasing frequencies of the colours. Red base is the lower energy with violet crown being the highest at this level. Now you imagine yourself walking out of the rainbow and along a shining path of

Light. In front of you there is a forest, and even as you approach it you can feel the welcome it extends to you.

A word here about imagination. You cannot imagine what is not. Some people are sceptical about this, which probably reflects a limited imagination! Your imagination is your creative factor. No animals can imagine. Remember, imagination is not all fantasy as we have always believed. Unrealised, you create your life, your world, with your imagination. In this exercise you use it for the same purpose. There will come a moment — you will never remember when — that your imagination will meet and merge with a greater reality . . . and your journey into Nature begins.

Just as it is our misguided and deluded imagination that holds us in our prisons, so it is the correct use of our imagination that will set us free. All the great sages, mystics, poets and renowned spiritual teachers throughout the ages have discovered this, each in their own time . . . and still it eludes the vast mass of humanity. Our imagination is a power that is misunderstood and misused by the general population. Sports psychologists, however, have learned exactly how to use imagination to the greatest benefit of their sporting clientele.

From here on it is practise, practise, practise. I listened to a young world-class pianist once talking about her practice. At three years of age she knew that she wanted to be a concert pianist. Her piano teacher told her that she would need to practise four hours a day until she was old enough to go to school. When she began school she should practice eight hours a day. She did this. At sixteen years of age she made her world debut in Carnegie Hall, New York. She gave all credit to the many, many hours of practice. It seemed to escape her that she was also a rather remarkable young lady.

One last issue. There is absolutely nothing to fear in this practice, yet it is the fear of the unknown that is the hideous strength of the prisons in which people live. I repeat, there is nothing to fear. Fear is False Evidence Appearing Real. It is never real, *always* false. Fear comes from the misuse of the imagination. Fear has no reality other than that which we give it. I have metaphysically journeyed very many times and

I have written several books detailing my adventures. Never have I had an encounter that I was not adequately prepared for. I have had shocks and many surprises, but fear has never been an issue.

Summary: We have now established the procedure that is required to be practised to actually enter the secret world of Nature. None of this is easy but, compared with piano playing, it is entirely natural. We were never designed to live only within the restraints of a physical body, nor were we designed to imprison ourselves and stay in these prisons of false beliefs and ignorance.

Be aware, however, that we have spent thousands of lifetimes in the prison of the physical body . . . yet it is not a prison, nor was it designed as such. As a Being of Light and Love you are able to *consciously* leave when you so wish. As an immortal Being, take all the time required.

Practise. Patiently practise. Practise patiently. Do not attempt to hurry the process or try to be clever. Do not underestimate yourself, but neither should you overestimate yourself. Allow your progress to be as natural and unhurried as the unfolding petals of a flower in the morning sun. You *are* an eternal Being!

Chapter Twelve

CHAOS — ORDER — BALANCE

Energy is the source of all growth. Physical or metaphysical, all growth is the result of the alchemy of energy. You could even say 'energies', implying that there is more than a single energy involved, but in the bigger picture this becomes a meaningless conjecture, because it makes no difference. Energy IS. Obviously, energy is not static; this is impossible. Energy creates its own dynamic. This is actually part of creation. You could even say it 'is' creation. In terms that you can comprehend, we will call that dynamic the torsion between Chaos and Order. Essentially, this endless torsion creates varying degrees of imbalance between Chaos and Order, an imbalance that is not easily affected by an outside influence. However, this torsion can be affected by human consciousness.

I have written about these basically unknown metaphysical principles in several of my more recent books, but if you are planning a foray into the secret world of Nature, then it will be to your benefit if they are studied even further. So let us begin at the beginning.

I am offering here the story of how I learned about what is probably the fundamental dynamic of the evolution of consciousness. I have never encountered any writing by any other authors that even vaguely approaches this — although they may exist. In all honesty, I think the academic world would once again mock me, but I am okay with this. The passage of time will prove that which I cannot. I have learned that the opening of our metaphysical eyes is a very slow process for people who believe that they can already see.

The following took place in 2005, while on a metaphysical journey with Pan. *(Through the Eyes of Love: Journeying with Pan, Book One)*

I was sitting in my study, reflecting on my own changing nature as I quite swiftly — okay, over *years!* — matured in my metaphysical journeying. Previously, I had been impulsive and headstrong and, without realising it, filled with the need of drama and trauma; this made it more real, more indelible. Any task that Pan set for me I seemed to perform with the maximum amount of pain and suffering, caused by my reluctance and resistance. Yet, over time and with Pan's ever-patient guidance, along with my perseverance, I came to that place of Truth, of spiritual enlightenment — the place where self is fully surrendered to Self.

My whole relationship with Pan had also changed. I once needed to see his metaphysical form from my own metaphysical reality, but slowly Pan had withdrawn that privilege. It was never real. It was a Pan image that Pan had somehow created in me, so that I could see him and be comfortable in this. But Pan showed me that comfort and stagnation hold hands, so all such supports had gradually been withdrawn as I became more and more certain of this greater reality — this secret world of Nature.

Thinking of Pan, I relax, giving myself to his ever-available energy. Changing my focus, as smoothly as water pouring from a glass, I move away from my physical body into my Light-body. With no hesitation, I am moving into that other dimension of life, of places and opportunities that are not based in a physical reality. Just as we have the physical world, so we have a non-physical invisible world; invisible to us, that is, on our slower bandwidth. To the Beings that inhabit this invisible reality, it is as real and visible as our world is to us. Much more so. In this moment I am being gently pulled into this other pristine world of Nature. Without having shape or form, I am spinning and twisting as I am drawn through this world of a tranquil Nature into an aspect that feels both raw and violent.

In a field of young wheat, I become aware of my Light-body. As I look around I am really puzzled. Not because it is wheat, for with years of farming background, wheat is very familiar to me, but this wheat is different. Wheat is growing over the whole field, but instead of being green, it seems to be flickering between shades of black and red. As I look closer, I see that the wheat is indeed green, but within that greenness, colours of red and black seem to be struggling for dominance. Brushing my fingers of Light over some blades of wheat, I realise that the colours are not physical. Physically, and of course, metaphysically, the young wheat is green, while the reds and blacks are somehow within the *energy-field* of each plant.

"What is this?" I ask Pan. Whereas I occasionally used to feel a bit abandoned by Pan if I could not see him, and very alone in some of my deeper metaphysical experiences, now I have the compensation of knowing that wherever I am, Pan is.

Do you not recognise a field of wheat when you see it?

Inner-feeling hints of laughter that are not my own, I quietly mutter about how the field is obviously wheat, but what is the red and black energy stuff?

Energy can be felt. So feel into it.

I sigh. Deep down I am not sure that I want to connect with that energy. Even without trying it feels . . . very disturbing. I gaze around, delaying.

Come on, Michael. If you can handle a storm, this should be easy.

I flinch at the memory (*Journey into Nature*). That had been a rather frightening experience, one that I did not wish to repeat. "Okay, so what am I supposed to do?"

Make a conscious connection with these energies. Be with it.

Silently, I groan. This is not something I want to do. Why, I do not know. I just know very strongly that I do not want to connect with those coloured energies. Is it my old reluctance, or something else?

Would you like my help?

"No, I definitely don't want your help. I know only too well that you'll simply throw me in. No thank you, I'll do it my way," I said hurriedly. Memories of the past roiled within me. I would rather ease my own way into this energy, the way I would tip-toe into a freezing-cold ocean.

As you wish.

Tiptoeing is easier said than done. Focusing on the flickering red colours, I reach out to them. I say *them* because the red is so full of shades and expressions of red that it feels more like a *them* than an *it*. For timeless moments I seem to be swirling all over the field of wheat, my Light-body under the influence of redness. As I stabilise, I feel the onrushing energy of total Chaos sweeping over me, and all stability is shattered. Nausea sweeps over me, but sickness in a Light-body is impossible. I think! The energy I feel is dynamic, a vast power that forces and compels, yet is neither negative or in any way wrong in its energy. It is reminiscent of when I was metaphysically within a storm, and yet hugely different, for I am not out of control. I feel myself to be bursting with unrestrained emotions, with uncontrollable intent, with a wildness that has never, ever, been tamed or tethered.

The feeling of nausea persists. This is the first time I have ever felt unwell in this non-physical world, and I feel off-balance, mentally thrown, muddled and jumbled, utterly chaotic, my Light-body also disordered. I do not like the feeling.

"Okay Pan, I feel thoroughly rotten. Now what?"

Since when have I spoon-fed you?

"I don't like this. I don't know what I feel. I can't focus. I hardly even know what I'm doing. I feel like swirling chaos."

Exactly. This is precisely what the red energy represents — Chaos.

"Oh! So what am I supposed to do with it?"

Nothing. There is nothing you can do with it, but you could try to maintain Balance.

Engulfed in this swirling, confusing, yet dynamic red energy, I attempt to regain my balance, my centre, but it is rather like trying to find heat in an iceberg. Forget balance, I cannot focus on anything. To attempt focusing is rather like trying to stabilise a whirlwind.

"Um . . . I can't," I say cautiously. Seriously, 'can't' is not a good word to use around Pan!

I can inner-feel Pan laughing. *Of course not.*

"So what is this all about?" I ask boldly.

93

I am going to show you life in farms and fields, in trees and forests, in mountains and hills, in towns and villages, in houses and homes, in wildlife and in zoos, in cities and humanity, in health and sickness, in anger and sorrow, and much more. Through my eyes you will see life as energy. The energy, of which you have just touched the very periphery, is Chaos, and Chaos is in everything that is physically made manifest on Earth. Neither good or bad, nor right or wrong, nor negative or positive, Chaos is pure energy.

I nod absently. "So if the colour red in all its shades is Chaos, common sense suggests that the flickering shades of black are . . . er . . . Order?"

Of course. What greater alchemy can there be than Chaos and Order. Are you ready?

"No! Er . . . ready for what?"

To experience Order, of course. What else?

What else indeed? I am still feeling as though I am the prey of some unseen spider, thoroughly wrapped in the silken strands of chaotic turmoil.

"Can you get me out of this? I'm not sure how to go about it."

Let go in any way that feels appropriate for you.

I mull his words over. There has got to be some hidden meaning here, but I cannot get my thoughts together enough to figure it out. Abruptly, my Light-body begins trembling, and then I am spinning round and around like a whirling dervish. To my delight, I can see the shades of redness flinging away from my Light-body, leaving me with my normal Lightness of Being. This feels so much better.

"Did I do that, or did you?"

Beyond thought, your own consciousness knew the solution. So, Order awaits.

The field of wheat remains and, as I metaphysically walk over it, I cannot help but wonder how the wheat feels about these energies of Chaos and Order. With the thought comes the knowledge that I am going to find out soon enough. I place my attention now on the flickering black colours that appear to dance and twist and whirl in a crazy, yet different, type of synchronicity with the red energy of Chaos.

As my attention is focused on the black energy, so it is attracted to me. My Light-body is swiftly becoming flickering shades of black, and oddly, everything seems to slow down. Only now do I realise that the red of Chaos had a speeding up effect, while the black of Order slows and controls, without *really* controlling. The sense of Order which is sweeping through me is very powerful. Literally, I can feel the *power* of Order. My own nature is drawn strongly toward everything in order, so I am feeling very much in harmony with it. Yet, as I am drawn deeper into the energy of Order, so it is becoming ever more s-l-o-w and p-o-n-d-e-r-o-u-s. I feel stilled and stifled by some abstract type of dogma. I feel the stars are in their courses, and I feel the rightness of this, but again the paradox: Order is neither right nor wrong, good or bad, positive or negative. In fact, just as with Chaos, on its own it feels to me as though Order would close the shop, putting it into order while all humanity was compelled to form a long orderly queue and wait endlessly for the shop to re-open. I knew it would never reopen; Chaos is, somehow, the dynamic that runs the shop.

Fascinated, I feel the bluntness of Order, knowing that the blunt edge of Order is sharpened on the rough stone of Chaos. Then, on a surge of new insight, I realise that Pan is the perfect Balance of Chaos and Order.

Once again I am whirling like a mad Being, swinging Order away from me in a way that I would never have contemplated. I like my personal type of order, but Balance is far more preferable.

"I have to admit, Order and Chaos are like nothing I would ever have imagined. I guess life is a process of bringing them into Balance."

Yes. Not an easy task when people have no awareness of Order and Chaos as universal energies — energies that permeate all life on Earth. Energies that for humans are under the control of human thought. Energies that can heal or kill. I could go on.

"I get the picture. But what about Balance? When do I meet this?"

We will leave Balance for your next excursion. Balance needs a bit of explanation. Also, it will be up to you to create it.

"Er, you mean my *own* balance?"

Of course. Where else is Balance except within Self and life in the moment?

Where indeed?

*   *   *

A few days pass by while I idly contemplate Balance.

One warm morning as I walk into our garden, I pause, one hand lingering on the newly smooth trunk of a grey gum. With many hundreds of species of Eucalyptus trees in Oz, we invariably take the easy way out, calling them gum trees. Grey gums are one of those trees that cast off their outer bark practically every year. Really messy! But what I love about these trees is their natural intelligence. In our subtropical climate, we should have wet summers and reasonably dry winters. This is normal. Unfortunately, *should have* and *normal* are no longer normal!

With climate change we often have dry summers and wet winters. However, if the summer is going to be dry, grey gums seem to be aware of this well before the summer begins. Forget the calendar seasons. For us, winter ends in early September and summer begins late September. Spring is a couple of weeks squashed in the middle. By October, and on through to November or December, the grey gums seem to have an innate knowing of the expected summer rainfall. If there will not be enough rain to precipitate new growth and expansion in the trunk of the tree, then the grey gum will retain its old, grey bark. If the expected rainfall will be enough for good growth, in November/December the grey gum will begin discarding its old bark in large thick sheets. And it does appear to be reasonably accurate! No matter what the long term forecasts are, my grey gums let me know whether it will be a wet or dry summer. So far!

Happily this year is wet, so the trunks of my grey gums are smooth and new. The new bark is a pale washed-out orange-ochre colour, but when wet it becomes such a startlingly vivid orange that a photograph at this stage looks completely unbelievable. It is only as the bark ages that the trunks fade to the familiar pale grey.

I love the natural intelligence of these trees. Some people raise their eyebrows when I describe the tree's ability to know whether or not it can grow over the next six months, as an act of intelligence. Note that I describe it as *natural* intelligence . . . as in Nature's intelligence. I am sure that science would dispute my choice of the word. From a metaphysical viewpoint, all Nature is an expression of intelligence, obviously including the animal, vegetable and mineral kingdoms. I am sure that some people would say that such an ability in a tree is no more than a biological process, not intelligence. I would reply that such thinking is no more than an intellectual process, not intelligence. Humanity needs to embrace and accept that it is natural holistic intelligence that shapes and maintains the universe, but this does require a fair degree of humility. And we are not big on that!

My hand on the tree, I stare up at it. It is so HUGE. I sometimes ponder on the fact that a tree is simply a big plant, yet when a large branch falls in a storm and I take hours to cut it up and cart it away, somehow a tree is no longer *just* a big plant. A really big tree takes on a status all of its own. I live on top of a small mountain ridge. People who live in mountainous countries would smile, and refer to it as a hill, yet although it is no more than hill in size, it is mountain in its energy. Grey gum trees like the tops of high hills and ridges. Walk down the mountain and the gum tree species change. Stringy-bark, black-butt, tallow-wood, plenty of varieties, but the grey gum has an attitude for altitude. I like grey gums. I do not mind them shedding their bark. After all, dogs bark and are constantly shedding!

The hugeness of a mature tree puts us people in our place. I'm sure this is an aspect behind the psychology of cutting down trees when we now have alternative sources of material for building. Human arrogance does not like looking up! The people who truly love and protect trees are not the arrogant types. They look up at a tree and enjoy the feeling of wonder, awe and humility that this produces. It puts us in our place. Not a place of 'less than', but a place of wonderment and awe. We need that.

I can feel the energy of the tree beneath my hand. Eyes closed, I let my sense of identity drift away, receding to some distant place. With others of its kind, this tree connects the conscious energy of Earth with the consciousness of the stars in ways we cannot even imagine. This tree has known me for about twenty years; it is familiar with my energy. It knows the Being I am. Trees do not relate to the human act, the petty little deceits we project to each other, they relate to our field-of-energy. They do not lay judgements on us, or pass messages to each other if we do not shape up; they simply allow our energy to open the doors of potential between ourselves and a tree, or to keep such doors tightly closed.

Although physically I am leaning against the tree trunk, metaphysically I am sinking into the tree. Just as I am physical and metaphysical, so also is the tree. The physical tree supports my physical body, the metaphysical tree opens to the metaphysical me. As I shift into my Light-body mode, flowing into the energy of tree, so I am again surrounded by those flickering shades of red and black.

I smile. Pan never misses an opportunity. In all the many times I have been into a tree, never once have I ever seen these shades of red and black.

You were never ready.

I have no doubt that this is perfectly true. It is all about timing.

"It would seem that I am ready now, but I don't really feel any different."

Let the tree show you your present energy.

"How can it do that?"

As I metaphysically move along the lines of tree energy, the flickering red and black colours become quieter, more subdued as I pass among them. All around me it is subdued light, and to my surprise I see another Being of Light flowing gracefully along the lines of tree energy. I stare in wonder. As this Being moves among the red and black colours, so they are transmuted into a dancing white Light. A paradox, for they are transmuted, yet they remain. Intuitively, I know the white Light is Balance. As I watch this Being, so it watches me. I raise one hand and smile, in the way I might greet a friend, and its hand is raised with the same smile coming back to me.

I gasp. This other Being *is* me! In some strange manner I am seeing my own reflection. It is I who am bringing Balance to the tree. How can this be? Do I have power over a tree, or am I able to convey my inner Balance to a tree? And through the tree into the universe? Is such a thing possible? I have a surge of questions.

This reveals the true role of humanity. You are the Light Bringers of Earth, or, failing this, you bring the shadows of despair. Either you add the Light to Truth, creating finite balance, or you clothe illusion in varying shades of deception, creating ever more imbalance between Chaos and Order.

"Is there no in-between? Couldn't we act in a way that affects neither balance or imbalance?"

How could this be? Adding your energy to life must mean that Chaos and Order is stimulated. Even though it is often unrealised, human energy always has a direction and purpose . . .

"But is there no choice in this?" I cut in. "Is it so cut and dried? Are you saying that our every action is either empowering Chaos or Order, or empowering Balance?"

Not Chaos or Order, Chaos and Order, and not just balance, but finite Balance.

"I'm getting confused. What exactly is Chaos and Order? And where did '*finite*' Balance suddenly come from. What happened to ordinary balance?"

Energy is the source of all growth. Physical or metaphysical, all growth is the result of the alchemy of energy. You could even say 'energies' implying that there is more than a single energy involved, but in the bigger picture this becomes a meaningless conjecture, because it makes no difference. Energy IS. Obviously, energy is not static, this is impossible. Energy creates its own dynamic. This is actually part of creation. You could even say it is creation. In terms that you can comprehend, we will call that dynamic the torsion between Chaos and Order. Essentially, this endless torsion creates varying degrees of imbalance between Chaos and Order, an imbalance that is not easily affected by an outside influence. However, this torsion can ...

"But this means that we are at the mercy of this . . . torsion."

Do not interrupt. Torsion is a deliberate design that can be affected by human consciousness.

"Sorry. So basically it is not about the degree of imbalance between Chaos and Order, it is about the balance of the person or people involved."

That says it well. However, in the frame of reality in which you physically live, the state of 'infinite' balance is not possible. This is why I refer to 'finite' balance. Finite balance is in direct relationship to your finite reality.

"Oh . . . that seems to make sense. What would represent infinite Balance?"

God. Metaphysical Nature.

"Ah, I think I understand. However, coming back to earth regarding Chaos and Order, does this mean that in our abusive modern agriculture Chaos is greater? It hardly seems possible to increase Order when we plunder the land. How do we create greater Order? It's obvious how we create greater Chaos. It would seem we do that naturally."

When Chaos is greater in the human consciousness then, Chaos increases in direct proportion within that person's field of energy, within their life. The same is true of Order.

"Well, that seems simple enough. The more Order we have, the more Order around us. Easy."

If it is so simple, demonstrate your ease at increasing the Order within this tree.

Hmm, now what do I do? Rather than try to do anything, I simply focus on the perfection and beauty of the tree, without attempting to add or subtract anything. I feel the movement of the energy within the trunk, and tentatively I imagine the Light within the tree becoming ever more illumined. Happily, it all feels beneficial and positive.

Very good, Michael. You took the right approach. Now you know what is meant by Light Bringers.

I smile to myself as the experience all melts away, and I am standing by the grey gum, my hand on its trunk. Truth is invariably simple, even if often profound!

Later, when I allow a greater insight to filter into me, rather than try to just mentally understand these astonishing principles that I have learned about, I am able to come to terms with them. It has become apparent that *Chaos is the engine that drives.* It drives growth and change, everything that to us is represented by life. *Order is the stability of structure.* It prevents plant and animal bodies — their very structure — from coming apart, or growing 'wrong'. It keeps things together, stable, but it does not generate growth. Chaos would tear everything apart if not for Order, and Order would deny all growth if not for Chaos. Together, within their torsion, they appear to be opposing energies. Yet, despite how it appears, they are in harmony, not opposition. A good example of pure Chaos is a wildfire, with zero Order. A granite rock is an example of Order, with almost zero Chaos.

As the energies of Chaos and Order are forever in torsion, swinging one way or the other, at the point of perfect tension is Balance. *Balance is the place of greatest potential.* If you — Order, and another person — Chaos, wring the ends of a wet towel in opposing directions, between you is created the energy of torsion. This is the energy that dispels the water from the towel. Too much torsion and the towel will collapse into two pieces; not enough and the towel will remain saturated. When the torsion is Balanced, the towel will be damp and dynamic, strong and energised.

As I stated in my Introduction, I capitalise the first letter of the *key* words, e.g., Chaos, Order and Balance, so that you will not be confused with the established meaning of these words. I am not describing our regular everyday chaos, or normal order and balance, I am writing of a principle that applies to our universe. It is difficult to describe metaphysical energies that have no physical translation . . . so I have to be creative. By capitalising Chaos/Order and Balance in this way, it is my intent to change the very ethos and character of the key words in this book.

The account I have shared is from an experience of about twelve years ago, and not unnaturally I have greatly expanded in my experience with Chaos, Order and Balance since then. I have found that just as we have our own individual states of consciousness, reflecting in our own varying states of Chaos, Order and mostly *lack* of Balance, so

101

this reflects in humanity as a whole. Now, in 2018, it is easy to see that globally, the Chaos of humanity is rising. These dynamic principles are the key factor of Change that is sweeping our planet. It is neither good nor bad, but it is *very* necessary.

In my experiences, the varying shades of reds in Chaos and the varying shades of black in Order are countless. When I talk of this I usually say a thousand shades of each colour, but this is more a feeling than an actual count. Every shade of red in Chaos has its own emotional connection within me as I experience it. It can range from deeply malignant to radiant joy. The intellect is left out in the cold, because this seems to be a purely emotional language. The same applies to Order. The emotional range is far beyond my ability to find words to describe it. Interestingly, all emotions are metaphysical, so such a language makes a lot of sense for the metaphysical Beings that we are. It is interesting to realise we have an immensely rich natural universal language of the emotions awaiting its time to emerge in the human consciousness. This is a language that reaches far beyond the limits of our present intellectual language: a language that is seriously deficient when it comes to discussing human emotions and a greater reality.

Summary: I have done my best to show you that the secret world of Nature is not something that you need to understand. You never will, for like 'peace' it is beyond understanding. Trust your experiences. If you get shocked, okay, you are shocked. Knowing that you have just hit an emotional block, you recover and move on.

You might ask, "Will Pan help me?" This is unanswerable. However, I will say, categorically, that you do not need Pan to assist you. All of us have the wherewithal in consciousness to be able to do this. There was a purpose in my encounters with Pan, and a reason that he is my mentor. (*Through the Eyes of Love, Journeying with Pan: Book Two,* Chapter One.)

We all have our own different approaches to Nature. For most people it is physical, sometimes skipping on the very edges of the metaphysical. For me it is physical in my much-loved garden, yet to a lesser degree it is also metaphysical. However, when I relax my physical body and move into a far greater metaphysical reality, then the physical becomes almost, but not quite, irrelevant.

Chapter Thirteen

MAKING YOUR CONNECTIONS

In that city park, I watched Nature/Earth energetically select and consciously connect with the people in the group who appreciated the park, its trees and its flowers, etc. Not for a moment am I suggesting that Nature/Earth made energetic judgements, or any such thing. What I saw was people who were open to Nature being connected without their realising it. Most of the people affected within the conscious connection were aware of this on a very hazy, non-intellectual level. They felt good. They smiled in the park, becoming more energised. The people for whom the park was just a shortcut — nothing. No energy of Nature went near them, no deeper connections took place. The few who found the park boring were unaware of being in a grey, low-energy fog, with absolutely no connection to Nature. In fact, strange as it may seem, they appeared to be de-energised. I later realised that this was self-created, as they inner-resisted their natural surroundings.

Apart from people like the Kalahari Bushmen and other so-called primitive tribes in their various countries, most of humanity has lost its conscious connection with Nature and the Earth. The results are dramatic, yet very little is known, recognised, or accepted about this. Let me shock you! Neither Nature nor the planet Earth acknowledges the living existence of a subconscious person. With over ninety percent of humanity living subconsciously, we unwittingly hold back the very evolution of human consciousness.

Every living creature in Nature is conscious in the moment, and in this we can include the mineral kingdom, thus involving the planet Earth itself. All Nature and the planet are conscious of consciousness. Obviously this is not on an intellectual level, but as a living reality. A person living subconsciously is not conscious of being conscious in the moment. Sounds odd, but it is a very sobering fact. It also has a very *startling* effect. I have viewed this effect by seeing through the eyes of Pan, and it took some time for me to fully comprehend the truth of what I was seeing.

Imagine a large group of people walking through a city park. For some it is a few moments of sanity away from the mindless, frenetic crowds; for others it is a short cut. Some few are feeling an inner love and gratitude toward the trees, the flowers, or whatever catches their attention in Nature. And for a few it is boring, no longer holding the excitement of the crowd- energy. There is no right or wrong to any of this; we are all different.

This, however, was how I first learned about human connections with Nature. I thought, I assumed, I took for granted that although many people do not even *like* Nature, that Nature and the Earth had no choice but to be involved in our individual and collective human consciousness. It seemed obvious to me that we were here, and like it or not, Nature/Earth was stuck with us! I was wrong.

In that city park, I watched Nature/Earth energetically select and consciously connect with the people in the group who appreciated the park, its trees and its flowers, etc. Not for a moment am I suggesting that Nature/Earth made energetic judgements, or any such thing. What I saw were people who were open to Nature being connected without their realising it. Most of the people affected within the conscious connection were aware of this on a very hazy, non-intellectual level. They felt good. They smiled in the park, becoming more energised. The people for whom the park was just a shortcut — nothing. No energy of Nature went near them, no deeper connections took place. The few who found the park boring were unaware of being in a grey low-energy fog, with absolutely no connection to Nature. In fact, strange as it may seem, they appeared to be de-energised. I later realised that this was self-created, as they inner-resisted their natural surroundings.

I have checked this out to reevaluate it many times, and there are no exceptions. I have even seen farmers, market gardeners and orchardists who had no connection to Nature or the Earth whatsoever, and they are working in Nature almost daily! How could this be? Because Pan would not assist me, it took me a quite while to find the most common factor. (Pan insists that I grow through my *own* observations!) I would like to add that these few disconnected farming people are the minority of all the various types of *true* farmers — men and women who are involved in real soil husbandry regardless of the crop. However, in our modern world of agribusiness this disconnection is far more common. For many there is no interest in an abundant margin of natural living nutrients in the land; their only concern is their abundant profit margin. I found it very disturbing that they had no conscious connection with Nature or the spirit of the land. What does it matter, you might ask, they still produce food?

Well, isn't that a good question.

It has become apparent to me that with the great mass of humanity involved in playing illusion games, it is unable to grow in consciousness. Human consciousness is not holistically growing, nor has it for a long time: hence planetary *Change* . . . a cosmic kick up the backside! Yes, there is clearly growth in consciousness in many of the more aware and conscious individuals, and that is millions of people, but in that *much* greater percentage of people who are subconsciously preoccupied, un-fortunately, no.

We are in a time of climate change, along with inner-Earth changes and many subtle changes taking place in Nature. By inner-Earth changes I mean that by metaphysical investigation, I have found that the great inner-Earth ocean of magma close to the Earth's core is heating up. This affects the tides, the great ocean currents, the melting of the icecaps from beneath, the trade winds, the high altitude airflow, our ocean tidal levels, the rivers . . . everything; and all life is affected, and is now un-dergoing Change.

If Nature/Earth has no recognition of a person as being conscious,

Nature will be utterly uncaring of their welfare . . . they are not part of a greater reality. And *a part is the whole, for there are no parts*! Equally, if Nature recognises a person as being One with its holistic Self, Nature will not wantonly or accidentally destroy a person with an aware connection of conscious intelligence.

I need to explain this. It would appear that in floods and storms, in earthquakes and cyclones many people are wantonly or accidentally killed. But this is a purely human viewpoint. Nature is the very *continuity* of life: no beginnings or endings. So while an aware, conscious, connected person could be seen to be physically killed and destroyed, on a metaphysical level they are consciously placed into a new environment more suitable to their own expanding consciousness. Of course, this will be seen outwardly as pure destruction, for changing to a higher bandwidth can, and may, cost the price of yet another physical body. Often, a de-structuring is required before a re-structuring can begin.

Can I prove any of this? Of course not, especially to a sceptic driven by fear and an unwillingness to see the greater reality. Again, all you have to do is journey into other realities and it all becomes apparent. Nothing, I repeat, *nothing* is by accident, *nothing* by chance. Everything that takes place in our lives is an act within the vast holistic aspect of the universal dance of creation. As Jesus said, "Not a sparrow falls . . ." Everything is in its perfect place in the most perfect order to achieve the most perfect growth in consciousness. I agree it may not *appear* that way when you look at life and humanity through the eyes of separation, but I can assure you it is so.

Okay . . . I recommend this daily practice to *consciously* reconnect.

In the pad of each foot there is a chakra. Since 2012, the potential of each foot chakra has increased considerably. At least twice a day, just stand on the planet Earth, pavement, grass, soil, wherever, and be aware of your thoughts. Slow them down and focus on the conscious *living* Earth beneath your feet. Feel the Light of Self flowing down through your feet chakras deep into the soil, making a *conscious* connection with the whole planet. Realise that wherever you walk on the planet you are not just in a country, in a district, in a garden or park on one little piece of the Earth, for the Earth has no parts. *Wherever you are standing or walking it is on the whole planet.* This is called being holistically conscious. In the moment that you consciously connect with the Earth, the Earth will consciously connect with you.

You do not have to remove your shoes and socks to connect. You could be at the top of a high-rise building with dozens of layers of plastic and concrete between you and the land, it makes no difference. The moment you *consciously* connect, nothing can prevent the connection. Hopefully, you have long ago realised that *consciously* is the key word, the key action!

Be aware that you cannot make this connection subconsciously. It can never be a habit. It can only ever be a conscious act of connection. Trust me on this, having the Earth energy consciously connected with the energy that is you is a very wise move. The Earth will give you conscious growth via the twice-a-day connection, and it will empower you with inner Balance as the physical aspect of our planet becomes increasingly erratic.

In a similar way, we have a chakra beneath the third finger in the pad of each hand. These also are more activated since 2012, with a greater potential. It is this activated chakra that many healers use. About twice a day, extend your hands out toward Nature and feel your Light Self energy flowing into and consciously connecting with Nature. The connection will be instant from Nature to you. In both the feet/Earth and hands/Nature connection, you are developing a *conscious* relationship that will be vital in the years of Change ahead of us. Be *consciously* connected.

I would like to reemphasise that we are a *seriously* disconnected species, although with many individual exceptions. Some people will have developed this conscious connection more recently, some will have made the conscious connection in other, 'previous' incarnations. This indicates that once your daily conscious connection is made, becoming a daily practice, then this vital connection will be implanted into your consciousness in such a way that it becomes part of your ever-growing reality.

Summary: You cannot admire a picture with your eyes closed. If you open your eyes and the picture is an abstract that defies all explanation to you, then you can see it, but you have no comprehension of its meaning.

In a similar way, people look at Nature but very few see. The physical bandwidth limits our ability to the extent we only see a tiny percentage of the full picture. However, when you *consciously connect* with the picture, you move to a new level of comprehension as the picture continually unfolds its greater reality into your open and developing consciousness.

Chapter Fourteen

SETTING YOUR INTENT

Intention has far-reaching benefits that many people are not aware of. An intention is, obviously, metaphysical. You could talk about it, but you could not physically show it to someone. An intention is the process of intentionally shaping your own metaphysical field of energy for the purpose of creation. Your energy-field is connected to the One energy-field of all life, indicating that you can, indeed, shape all life to your will . . . to a degree! For most people in denial of their power, that is a very, very tiny degree.

I have been asked, "Is there any difference between intention and goal setting?" Some people would say that there is little to no difference, but I see it rather differently. Goal setting is very linear, with a direction, a clear goal, and a time factor. Goal setting is very material oriented, and very much locked in to the physical world. It is also ego and self-will driven. And all this is perfectly okay.

If you set a five- or ten-year goal, and you do it correctly with focus, you will quite probably be much the same person after five or ten years as when you created the goal. In the process of reaching your goal you may actually have restricted your greater potential. However, if you grow in consciousness during the five- or ten-year process, then, when the time is up and you arrive at your goal, it will seem trite and pointless. The goal will no longer fit the growth of your consciousness.

So please, do not do set any goals or time factors if you are seeking to enter the secret world of Nature; it will not work in your favour.

However, I encourage you to create and take into your consciousness a very clear intent: that you *do intend* to enter the secret world about which I am writing. People are very different in their approaches and attitudes. Just reading this book and realising that self-discipline is required, and having to *consciously* practice to make a connection is too much for some people. They will have thoughts a bit like: I tend to procrastinate; I really can't do this; I'm put off by the required self-discipline; Wow, you *mean* I can't do this with a cellphone? (Joke!) I'm really too busy for this; I like the idea of it . . . but! Er, is there an easier way? Sorry, it all sounds just too difficult. There are so many reasons why, for some types of people, just reading this book is off-putting. However, reading this book may also sow a seed in their ready-to-grow consciousness that will have its own timing to develop and grow. If this is you, so be it. For most people, it almost sounds too simple to be true! But they also realise, of course, that simple is powerful!

Intention has far reaching benefits that many people are not aware of. An intention is, obviously, metaphysical. You could talk about it, but you could not physically show it to someone. An intention is the process of intentionally shaping your own metaphysical field-of-energy for the purpose of conscious creation. Your energy-field is connected to the One energy-field of all life, indicating that you can, indeed, shape all life to your will . . . to a degree! For most people in denial of their power, that is a very, very tiny degree.

Once you have consciously set your intention to consciously connect with Nature, you let it go free. It is now in the ethers: that metaphysical field of energy that precedes all physical manifestation. Your intent is now in your own field of energy, apparent of all life *beyond* the physical bandwidth. The inner movement/moment that a seed begins to germinate and grow is beyond our physical reality; it is purely metaphysical. We physically see it when it reaches our more familiar bandwidth. So it is with you and me. You have sown the seed of intent, and you are now required to follow through with the practise of that intent.

You bring into your daily life the practices that you are reading about and you *consciously* practise them. Always the key is being *conscious* of your focus, of your actions, even of your thoughts. *Thinking* about this as being difficult will result in the process being difficult . . . you are the creator! *Confident* thoughts of your innate ability to do this, simply because you are a metaphysical Being, will greatly assist you in doing it . . . you are the creator!

Nature reads our intent constantly and endlessly. If we were aware of the intent of another person to hurt us, feeling threatened, we would either put distance between us, or defend ourselves. Yet if a woodsman goes into a forest with the intent of felling a certain tree, although the tree knows his energy of intent the moment he forms it, the tree remains passive. You may think it has no choice — I agree — but the tree is not threatened. It has no relationship with death and endings, or pain and aggression. For the tree, it is as it is, and tree life will continue with or without the physical form.

Animals read our field of energy constantly; just occasionally we can read theirs. If a dog is snarling at us, we read the physical body expression. But if the dog simply gives us a mere glance, yet will bite when given the first opportunity, we have no idea of this. We 'read' animals more on a physical posture level than on its energy; the animal does almost the reverse of this. Our pets are constantly reading our ever-changing energy. Generally, people with pets love and adore them, and all too often spoil them rotten with over-feeding and over-pampering. This, of course, does not apply to you! I am sure you do not overfeed them because you are probably more aware. Okay, joking aside, many of us are inclined toward over-indulging our pets. And our pets are inclined toward over-feeding and becoming fat. In this pet/human equation, food and emotions are almost synonymous. Animals that would not over-eat under normal conditions will often over-eat under the emotional confusion of love equals food and food equals love.

Animals easily pick up on our energy and then act upon it. In a pet shop, I observed a person admiring a large cockatoo. We both saw the shop owner pick it off the perch and cuddle it, then putting it back, he stroked it. Very hesitantly, the admirer reached out to stroke the cockatoo . . . and got a severe peck! He grinned at me. "Just what I expected," he said, sucking his finger. The cockatoo knew that he was partially afraid of it, and human fear always gets attacked or rejected in Nature.

It is difficult for us to comprehend that we are continuously emitting and communicating via our field of energy to every living thing around us. We cannot see it ourselves, we do not see or feel it from other people — except in extreme cases — so we completely overlook it, or we do not know that this is happening. Add to this, most people are a walking mass of confused thoughts and emotional turmoil, unknowingly communicating this energy to the world. However, Nature is connected, listening, feeling and often reacting. Pets get used to this, along with farm and zoo animals. Wild animals are seriously spooked by it. Inner clarity and calm is a requirement for making meaningful connections with a Nature that extends far beyond just pets and domesticated animals.

Years ago a married couple, who were close friends of mine, lived in an outer suburb of Brisbane. They owned a dog named Nicky. Nicky was a mutt. He was of average size and so shaggy that if he stood still you had to look twice to know which end was which! He was good-natured and very friendly; a great pet and a faithful mutt.

It was Nicky's habit to go out into the garden about ten o'clock at night and check that all was safe and well for his human family. As far as he was concerned, Nicky was the protector of the family. One night, when they called him indoors soon after ten o'clock, he did not show up. They were not overly-concerned, calling him again at about eleven o'clock. No Nicky.

At this stage, Mike went out looking for him. He found Nicky lying near a window, his skull broken and bleeding, with one eye hanging out of its socket onto his cheek. He was rushed to the vet as an emergency. The good news is that Nicky survived, minus one eye . . . neither of which you could see under his shaggy fur anyway! With patience and observational skills, Mike pieced together the story of what happened to Nicky.

Apparently, a man had attempted to jemmy a window open with intent to burgle the family home. It appears that Nicky interrupted this and the man hit him with the jemmy bar. Nicky fell over and bled. The man then shifted his attention to another window in the rather big house. It would seem that Nicky staggered to his feet and again attacked the man, this time receiving a heavy blow across the skull that knocked him unconscious. Twice disturbed, the man ran away.

The point of this story is intent. The intent of the man was to do harm to the family by burglary. Nicky knew this intent from the man's energy-field, so he did his duty and defended his family. If I had tried to get in as a family friend, Nicky would have probably tried to assist me.

Summary: I absolutely encourage you to consciously set your intention with regard to your relationship with Nature. Be very clear about your intention. Do not be ambiguous, or indecisive, or unsure, or unclear. Consciously inner-state your intention very clearly and be aware that you are communicating with all Nature and the Earth. This intention will guide you via your growing insights and intuition.

Be aware that your intent is not static. It is not a case of once it is stated you can forget it. You *live* your intent. If you live subconsciously, your intent will lose energy. If you remain *conscious* of your intent, and live it, then you empower your intent and your intent will empower you.

Chapter Fifteen

AVOIDING PITFALLS

Imagine having a bow and arrow, and a target. The target is Connecting with Nature. The bow is named Desire, while the arrow is Trust. You place the arrow in the bow and draw it back to tension. You aim at the target with Focus, then release the arrow. The flight of the arrow is Trust in action. From this point forward you hold your Focus on the target — Connecting with Nature — and you Trust. This works.

Many people go through the early part of the procedure, but in the moment the arrow is released they forget about Trust. Instead, they grab the arrow and attempt to guide it toward and into the target. By doing this they create attachment. Once attachment comes into the equation, all is lost. Some people spend many lifetimes running with the arrow, no longer knowing what they are doing, or where they are going, or even what that long-ago target was, or is. This does not work.

There are several major pitfalls that people can easily blunder into whilst attempting to enter the greater reality of Nature. Most of these have been mentioned throughout this book, but they deserve to be categorised and good working solutions offered. After much thought about this, I will place 'fear' at the top of all the possible pitfalls.

Fear is not easy to deal with. Fear has its own language, often a violent and angry one, but always disturbing. But fear also has a quiet and more subtle language of undoing, of bleeding away your inner potential and courage without your ever realising it. As I have written, fear is not natural in Nature. Indeed, human fear does not exist in Nature, even though we humanise what we see in the natural world and conclude that there is fear in Nature. Wrong.

You are going to need to make some choices here. You either doggedly persist in creating fear by misuse of your imagination and then attempting to overcome or fight your own creation, or you make the effort to *not create* fear in your life. Most people will do the former, even while preferring the latter. Sounds crazy, I know, but fear is a reaction and most people are locked into reaction modes throughout their life.

I am sure you will have fully realised by now that you really and truly cannot enter the secret world of Nature purely on techniques. To go into an ordinary room you need only open the door and walk in. The secret world of Nature is no ordinary room, and it has no ordinary door. The way into this room is to *know* that you have lived within it forever, but you have been very deeply asleep, dreaming that you were awake — the illusion. I am offering you the keys to awakening that slumbering giant within. We live our lives as deluded pygmies, yet we are so much more. To consciously enter this room of Nature requires you to become the Being you *are*, letting go of the person you think you are. While this book offers you a process of *conscious* inner transformation . . . for many, the unknown comes wrapped in fear.

If you go through this transformation, it will take you away from the familiar illusion and open you to an unknown reality. For humans, the unknown so very often engenders fear. Of course, we create this fear simply because we fear that which is not familiar to us; thus we avoid the unknown, thus we avoid inner change and growth, thus we avoid our divine potential . . . and on and on! You get the picture? You cannot change and remain the same! I am offering you change. I am offering you the death of sameness. You will feel some of these little deaths and you will be faced with more choices: fear or faith, newness or sameness, to inner grow or inner stagnate. This is when you need to remind yourself that you do not grow by outside stimulus unless you create the outside stimulus needed to kick-start your inner growth. You are the creator of your life, its content, and its direction. You grow or you stagnate . . . and more-of-the-same is stagnation.

All the techniques that you may have on defeating fear will simply give it more energy. Fear is an illusion, and you do not fight illusions because this feeds them with your energy. You *know* that fear drains you of energy; now you know how and why. You withdraw your energy from illusions by focusing on the Truth and beauty in your everyday life — and it is always there.

Another deep pitfall is attachment.

Because this book is about entering the secret world of Nature, I will keep my commentary on attachment to this. After reading my books, it is apparent that many people develop a strong desire to be able to experience a metaphysical Nature in a way similar to mine. Desire and attachments hold hands. We desire what we are attached to or we attach ourselves to what it is we desire. One of the greatest sources of self-suffering is through our attachments. To be *attached* to the desire of experiencing a metaphysical Nature is a way of ensuring that it will never happen.

Imagine having a bow and arrow, and a target. The target is Connecting with Nature. The bow is named Desire, while the arrow is Trust. You place the arrow in the bow and draw it back to tension. You aim at the target with Focus, then release the arrow. The flight of the arrow is Trust in action. From this point forward you hold your Focus on the target — Connecting with Nature — and you Trust. *This works.*

Many people go through the early part of the procedure, but in the moment the arrow is released they forget about Trust. Instead, they grab the arrow and attempt to guide it toward and into the target. By doing this they create attachment. Once attachment comes into the equation, all is lost. Some people spend many lifetimes running *with* the arrow no longer knowing what they are doing, or where they are going, or even what that long-ago target was, or is. *This does not work.*

At this point we bring in another pitfall: expectations.

Be aware that these pitfalls all interweave with each other. None of them stand alone. Many people come to one of my 5-Day Intensives with hidden expectations. During our conversations they make comments, "Wow, it was far better than I expected." Or, "It was completely different from what I expected," These, and other similar comments, made after having told me they had *no* expectations! They truly believed they were open, but hidden deeper were the expectations that they did not have! This is how easily we fool ourselves with the content of our deep subconscious.

If you take expectation into your attempts to enter the secret kingdom, you will invariable be disappointed. No expectations, no attachments, no desires. Remember the bow named Desire. As soon as the arrow is released, let go of the bow. Throw it away. For as long as you remain attached to Desire you will have expectations, and between them they will create more disappointment. All you need is a focus on Connecting and Trust.

Yet another pitfall is a lack of patience.

Patience is very misunderstood. So, what is patience? Patience is active and dynamic; it is not just waiting for something to happen. Patience is the participation in allowing the perfect timing to emerge. You wish to connect with Nature on a deeper level. Is it your timing? A bud goes through its necessary development until the moment it is ready to unfold into a flower. It is *never* a hurried process. Too much rain or drought can hinder it, but in perfect timing the flower will be revealed. An egg only hatches in perfect timing, according to the species of bird. A baby human or animal is born after the gestation period of the species. Everything in Nature follows timing, yet we tend to ignore it. We get impatient.

If you spend a day sitting with a rock you will find that Nature is incredibly patient. If you spend enough time on a mountain, or a solitary boulder — I prefer these — or by a meandering river: (my choice!) you will learn what patience truly is. When you connect with timelessness, you tend to become more patient. Many people live their lives filled with rush and hurry. These are not good companions for you. Patience and tolerance will take you on a much more meaningful journey, whereas rush and hurry will offer only the most superficial of lives. Even in an emergency ward in a hospital, while rush and hurry are often necessary they also need to be married to a calm inner focus, accompanied by trust. This works. It is all choices!

At this point let us marry patience with timing. Only you know if you have a *heart longing* to connect with Nature, or a want based in the so-called glamour of being different. If want is pushing you, I suggest that this is not yet your timing. When you have a deep, quiet, inner longing to connect with the greater reality of Nature, almost craving this nurturing connection, your timing has arrived. The timing in humans is always based in your consciousness. Unlike a bud or an egg, we create the timing of our timing! The more you inner grow, the more ready you are to expand beyond the limits of the physical bandwidth. Considering that you are a magnificent metaphysical, multidimensional Being, this is your birthright.

Another pitfall is your need to understand.

I have touched on this before, but I cannot stress the importance of *trusting* way beyond your need to understand. To reduce experience to fit into your limited understanding is to ensure failing in this connection. I long ago learned to trust beyond anything I understood in my many metaphysical journeys. What or who do you trust? You trust the magnificent, metaphysical, multidimensional, immortal Being of Love and Light who is the true Self. This is where you place your trust — in self/Self.

Please get this. If I spoke to you in Sanskrit — I cannot! — you would probably not understand me. If you focused on my energy, rather than my words, with practice you would take in a lot of what I said from a very different energetic level. With practice you would comprehend my intent and meaning whilst still having no understanding of my words. This is how it works on a metaphysical level in Nature. You have the potential for an entirely natural heart — whole-brain — intuitive connection that, in truth, far transcends our limited intellectual understanding.

Summary: These are a few of the pitfalls. I could talk of self-doubt, of a lack of self-worth and quite a few other human shortfalls, but if you have too many of these it indicates that you are not yet ready. And that is okay. Be aware that the whole journey is a learning process and that, although timing is important, there is never a time when you will de-clare yourself as perfect and ready. We simply do not operate that way! For me, self-doubt was a constant companion for all the early years of my journeying. Gosh . . . to be honest I think I probably had every doubt ever invented. *But I kept on keeping on.*

Chapter Sixteen

COMMUNICATING WITH NATURE

I focus on what it is that I am communicating with. It may be a tree or an animal that I can easily see, or it may be a river or mountain that I cannot physically see. I very seldom attempt to communicate with something in Nature that I have not physically seen or touched. If someone said to me that they have a magnificent tree in their garden that has told them it needs to communicate with me — yes, such things happen! — I am unable to make any connection. That tree has no living reality for me since I have never seen or in any way connected with it. We have no prior relationship.

How do I communicate with Nature? This is such a common question. How indeed? Naturally enough, I can only answer this from my own perspective. I have never discussed techniques with any other people who communicate with animals or trees. I certainly doubt that they communicate in a completely different way, but I cannot be sure.

As I have already stated, for me, it is all about listening. It is about closing down the mind chatter and being inner quiet. When we listen in a way that transcends outer hearing, the ears of the heart open. Of course, these are not actual 'ears', but in a similar manner, we inner hear at a deep, heart level, and we inner connect with a flow of communication.

At this stage doubt comes leaping in! "Is it my mind, or is this real?" you may ask? Doubt is a powerful adversary, and one that you do not need. Inner trust is the only way through this. Once you begin a dialogue with doubt, it will engage your attention for a long time. In my early days of communicating with Nature I had some *very* long conversations with doubt. They were entirely nonproductive, a complete waste of time, but I had to go through them simply because I was on my own. There were no books on the subject in those days, and I had nobody with whom to discuss it. It was a very lonely place!

In my early days, I struggled with people accepting the words and experiences that I would eventually write about in *Talking With Nature*. In truth, it was me who doubted my own experience; it was me who was struggling. I seemed unable to find a way around the problem. I would sit by the river day after day mocking myself with my own doubt-thoughts. The river spoke to me often, but each time self-doubt destroyed the communication. But, I persevered.

One day, I was watching an Eastern Water Dragon stalking a beetle that was on the end of a long, thin branch over the water. I figured that the branch was too thin for the dragon and that it would never reach the beetle. Sure enough, just as it closed in . . . the dragon fell off. I was fully engaged in watching this little drama, when the words of the river swept into me.

Do as the dragon did. Let go and fall into the river. Let the river of life sweep you beyond all aid from old and worn concepts, beyond all doubts. I will support you. Trust me. As you swim from an old consciousness, blind to higher realities beyond your physical world, trust that I will guide you with care and love into a new stream of consciousness. I will open a new world before you. Can you trust me enough to let go of the known, and swim in a new and unknown current?

As I struggled with what I was receiving, a cloud swept overhead making the river appear dark and forbidding. I had an inner sense that I was the dark cloud, or that it represented my doubts. It occurred to me that I either accepted and moved on, or I quit. I needed to move one way or the other.

In that moment I made my choice. I would trust. As I did this, the sun was suddenly shining on the river and me, the ominous dark replaced by a rippling river of light, sun-filled reflections.

I would like to say that all doubt ended then and there, but this would not be true. It was, however, the beginning of the end of my time of doubting. The point of telling you all this is so that you know that, if you should have self-doubt, it need not destroy your progression. Just move on through it with endless patience and boundless trust!

As I write about this, I am suddenly confronted by just how difficult it is to share the art of inner communication with you. It is rather like a child learning to walk. They just do it, some slowly after plenty of crawling or bum-shuffling, while others simply get up and take their first faltering steps.

For me, I focus on what it is that I am communicating with. It may be a tree or an animal that I can easily see, or it may be a river or mountain that I cannot physically see. I very seldom attempt to communicate with something in Nature that I have not physically seen or touched. If someone said to me that they have a magnificent tree in their garden that has told them it needs to communicate with me — yes, such things happen! — I am unable to make any connection. That tree has no reality to me since I have never seen or connected with it. Once I have connected in any country with an aspect of Nature, then no matter how many years pass, that connection is with me in the immediate moment.

In all this, focus is very important. Focus is not about focusing your eyes, it is about focusing your thoughts and giving your whole attention to whatever it is you wish to communicate with. Personally, I strongly feel that after you have read this book, gaining a clear insight into your required state of relaxed consciousness, along with the clear knowledge of what does and what does not work for you, you will be rather surprised at just how easy it actually is. Like smiling, you just do it!

So . . . I sit in my study and close my eyes. Yes, you can sit out in a physical Nature if it helps you, but after enduring years of mosquito and midge bites, of intense discomfort with pins and needles when my legs lost their blood flow, and of various other discomforts — none of which helped me one little bit — I surrendered to the comfort of my study chair. I would also emphasise that your communication is meta-physical, not physical; a non-physical you with the non-physical subject of your intent. However, if I was communicating with an animal for a specific reason, then I would sit close by it or in physical contact. Questioning a sick dog or cat, for example, hoping to gain an insight into the *cause* of the problem, or sickness, then by all means make it close and connected. This does not mean that it could not be a more distant communication, but for me, I would need to know the cat or dog involved. With that factor I could do it, but I prefer contact or close proximity with animals, especially if they have an issue. I am sure that many animal communicator specialists are not as limited in this as I am!

With my eyes closed, I focus on my subject. To be honest, I mostly leave my physical body these days and just wander out into a greater reality. I am now entirely comfortable with this. Sometimes Nature will attract my attention, sometimes Pan will engage me, and occasionally I am whisked away and suddenly involved in another life-expanding experience. I tend to allow that which is most appropriate in the moment to engage me . . . but it was not always this way. I have been doing this 'stuff' for a *very* long time!

If I am going to communicate only, my eyes are closed and I am focused on my subject. I will do this right now. I am focusing on the group of bonsai just outside my study window. Four of the large *ficus* — fig — are in a group to showcase their beauty, while the others live on the one metre high, flat-top wall around the large goldfish pond that I built. These are *ficus* and *bougainvillea*. Most of the *ficus* I have had for over forty years, so they are very familiar with my energy. The colourful *bougainvilleas* are comparative newcomers.

My focus is strongly attracted by the Strangler Fig. This is an old friend. Now, quite large and powerful, it began life with me as a mere sprig, with just a couple of small leaves.

Suddenly a flow of communication moves into me.

I/we wish to communicate about your concern with clearly and concisely communicating with other humans. True communication is an exchange of energy. You and I exchange this energy on a regular basis. Every time you water me, we exchange energy, even though you are not always conscious of this. You cannot act toward me in any way without spon-

soring an energetic communication. Today you are considering cutting back my leading shoots so that I can retain my shape, rather than grow shapeless and random. This is your art of bonsai. I, although not separate and not even an 'I', do not object to this, even though I/we do appreciate it when you communicate your intent.

In a like manner I/we suggest that you share your intent with the humans that you wish to engage. Focus on the humans as though they are many trees in a large and very diverse forest, all connected by Love and your clear, focused intention.

"Okay. Wow, I confess, I am surprised by this."

You should communicate to other humans that your language is no more than energy. When you and I/we merge in consciousness I/we nudge you toward the words that will best express my/our intent. You are certainly free to pick your own words in translating my energy into your human language, but do not underrate the natural energy of communication that is within all Nature. We do not struggle with words or concepts. We are able to communicate our intent very powerfully. This, of course, happens on many levels. Humans are familiar with pheromones in animal communication, but they are seldom aware of the power of energetic intent that accompanies this. We of Nature 'always' communicate with clarity, while you of humanity seldom have your words energetically aligned with clarity and true intent.

"I thank you most sincerely for this unexpected and welcome insight."

To be quite honest, dear reader, this communication is a big surprise to me. The level and depth of insight is obviously within me, but this bonsai friend is absolutely the prompter and the empowerment of the words that are chosen and used in this unexpected communication. Sure, I instigated the conversation, but, trust me, the content was entirely unexpected.

So I will eventually sit back and do exactly as suggested. I will imagine you reading this book . . . and smiling at these words. I will do my best to imagine you connecting with Nature in a meaningful way, and accepting it. One of the ways that greatly assisted me in my early days was the content of the shared communication. If I was receiving communication from a flower, or tiny moss, or a huge tree — whatever — I would always be aware if this was either old knowledge for me, or was *something that I did not know*. This would excite me. If I had no previous knowledge of what was shared, then how could my mind be playing games? This worked for me.

Today, I have a deep and vast knowing compared with those early years of doubt, and I no longer use this 'I knew, or I did not know' technique. But I still occasionally get surprised as just happened while writing this book.

Remember also, that because animal communication is an exchange of energy, it is the mind that will translate the energy of the communicating animal or plant into your words, and into your way of using them. If you are French all your animal communications will be in French, even if you are in England. Of course, animals do not have many different languages, they communicate with the language energy of Oneness. Notice that I do not write of animals speaking; they do not speak. They energetically communicate. Paradoxically, we often speak to each other with very little to zero energetic communication. Equally, a person speaking with passion creates a powerful energetic connection with his or her audience, be it one person or hundreds.

A Facebook friend named Bernadette sent me this little communication she had with a butterfly. Simple . . . but very powerful.

"Good morning, Michael. I would like to share an experience I had today. I was on my morning walk through the bush when I noticed a butterfly that looked as though it was dead. I picked it up and its wings fluttered so I kept it on my hand while I continued walking. Previous to this I had been thinking about the layers of myself that keep coming up for me to release. I forgot about all this as I was walking with the butterfly. I knew he had very little time left before he was once again non-physical. I also knew it had a message for me, so I quietened my mind, waiting for what this message might be. It said: *Butterflies breathe in joy then breathe out joy, whereas humans breathe in joy and breathe out pain.*

"I found a lovely place to put it, and as I walked away I began to cry. I then realised I was doing exactly what it said, breathing in joy and breathing out pain. I stopped crying and I was filled with joy. I know joy will now be my forever out-breath. Have a great day because I know I will!"

Summary: As Bernadette wrote, "I quietened my mind" . . . and she *listened.* Although you may consider yourself ready to communicate with some aspect of Nature, this does not mean or imply that Nature is ready to communicate with you. Nature reads you easily. If the intent and conscious energy is in balance it will most probably happen. However, if you are out of balance with desire or an attuned to an egotistical energy, the communication often will not happen. I experienced this quite often in my early years.

I will reiterate once more: everything is energy and all energy is information. The energy of information does not withhold information, or just share it with the deserving or the clever. This natural energetic information is available to anyone at anytime. This is true with everything that is natural on our planet and with all of Nature. All that you are required to do is to still the busy mind, then consciously connect . . . and listen.

"That's all," he said!!!

Chapter Seventeen

HUMAN INTERPRETATION
OF NATURE

I can definitely state that experiences change with your ever-increasing experience. My early imbalanced and frequently quite emotional years of communicating with Nature were rather different to my experiences of today. I strongly suggest that you let go of your many interpretations of Nature. Just be still and quiet in the moment. All that speculation and interpretation is nothing more than your intellect and your emotions attempting to understand, seeking the comfort of the known and familiar. To do this they create a nice, acceptable story. Let it go; you do not need it.

We are inclined to see Nature through the eyes of our education, along with those people who had the greatest influence on us as children. This very strongly sets the scene of our future experiences. As a generalisation, a boy growing up in a family that was strongly critical and sceptical of anything metaphysical or out of the ordinary, will very likely become a closed, cynical and very disbelieving man about all such things. The opposite is also equally true. The children of parents who are open to all things metaphysical will mostly grow up to be open-minded adults. Of course, there will be exceptions to this, but it is almost scary how easily we can be moulded when young into ways that will greatly limit, *or* increase, our later experiences of life. We can, of course, make our own more aware choices when we are an adult, rejecting or accepting our earlier childhood programming.

Add to this our very many different personality types. From the down-to-earth to the flighty airy-fairy types of people, all this has a great influence on our experiences with Nature. A woman sees the limbs of trees swaying and moving in the wind as highly emotional, very dramatic, finding a deep and disturbing human correlation in this, while to a male companion they are simply branches swaying in the wind. Obviously, there is no right or wrong to this, no should or should not . . . it is as it is. But if they both, each in their own timing, open the door to the secret world of Nature, they are obviously going to encounter very different experiences. And then imagine they later attempt to verbally share their experiences with each other, each looking for the comfort of validation from the other!

In a Metaphysics of Nature seminar I once asked each participant to go out into the nearby wood and find a tree with which they identified. It was quite an eye-opener. A strong-looking man identified with a sturdy oak. A quiet slender woman found a willow tree on the outer edge of the wood, near a stream. One woman chose a broken and deformed tree. When I questioned the various people about their choices, I learned that the man, like an oak, was strong but rather inflexible. The quiet woman with the willow lived on the edge of society, not liking crowds. The woman who chose a deformed tree worked with mentally and physically handicapped children.

It is quite common for some people to humanise Nature to the extent that they see fears in isolated trees, with camaraderie among clusters of trees, and also shock, loss, compassion, empathy and similar emotions in trees in a general way. Some people completely believe that a small copse of trees are Grandmother tree, Grandfather tree, Mother tree and Father tree, and the younger junior trees as their children. Some people consider a forest of trees as rather like an immobile herd of horses or cattle, with many fears and worries moving through and among them.

There was a time that I would have poured scorn on such people, but nowadays I smile and suggest that they seek to experience the isolated tree, or the copse, or forest. I am very aware that our past and our beliefs will hugely influence our metaphysical experiences, just as our past and our beliefs hugely influence our everyday life. Emotional people will almost always create emotional experiences, finding validation in their emotional beliefs. But is this right or wrong, you might ask? It is neither right nor wrong; it is as it is. Today I would never judge the metaphysical experiences of another based on my own experiences. If I am being told an account by a person, I listen to their energy as well as to their words. Each may tell a rather different story.

In every moment of your life you are creating the direction and the content of every moment of your life — physically and metaphysically. This implies that a person having a metaphysical experience will, on some level, be determining the outcome based on their openness or deep-seated beliefs. The more open they are, the less they influence the outcome. Based in my knowing this, how could I deny or even confirm another persons experience?

I can definitely state that experiences change your experience. My early, imbalanced and frequently quite emotional years of communicating with Nature were rather different from my experiences of today. I strongly suggest that you let go of your many interpretations of Nature. Just be still and quiet in the moment. All that speculation and interpretation is nothing more than your intellect and your emotions attempting to understand, seeking the comfort of the known and familiar. To do this, they create a nice, acceptable story. Let it go; you do not need it.

I am now going to write briefly of the emotions in Nature. This is an area of extreme controversy. Unfortunately, science made us familiar with the word anthropomorphism, meaning that people identified animals with humans. This, in turn, frightened many researchers, so their studies tended to lean in the opposite direction. Thus controversy regarding animal emotions as opposed to human emotions reigned supreme. I have read some very strong arguments both for and against emotions in animals. So, be warned. Most animal behaviourists research the animals and their emotions very carefully, then they make rational decisions on what they think the results of their studies and tests indicate. I have no argument with any of their results.

I am going to share with you *my metaphysical experiences* regarding emotions in Nature. Whether it contradicts your opinion or verifies it ... so be it. Whether it opposes popular belief, or supports it ... so be it. I can only be true to my own experiences of emotions in animals. Along with this, I have a request: please do not read these words about emotions in Nature and jump to conclusions. I *know* that many people at a talk hear what they want to hear, not necessarily what is said. They translate the spoken words into a validation of their beliefs. Equally, many people will read a book in exactly the same way, twisting the meaning and translating words to fit into, and verify their often very different beliefs.

Just be open; this is all I ask of you.

I have metaphysically journeyed into Nature for several decades. I have been within the consciousness of single trees, of the few-tree copses, of the English woods, of American forests and Australian rain-forests. I have been within the consciousness of many animals and birds ... and I have written many books about these experiences. In all these journeys I have never encountered any single trees or groups of trees that claimed to be families. They do not even have a concept of this; it is not in their reality. It is an emotional, human, projected perception. As I said, we tend to create and even hear whatever will validate our beliefs. Many years ago I also did the same; thus I learned of our human fallibility. Now, when I metaphysically journey, I am aware of this. We are full-time creators, not part-time!

Trees experience a conscious connection in a way that we know nothing of. No tree experiences itself as alone, or individual, or as a tree identity. All trees know themselves as multiple expression of One tree consciousness. Of course, this is not an intellectual knowing. It is intrinsic to the collective consciousness of trees. We can metaphysically touch into this, easily misinterpreting and translating it into our own beliefs and expectations. This is what some people close to Nature re-peatedly do.

I have never encountered any human emotion in any tree or trees. Our emotions are utterly unique to us. I have detected the faintest of very, very rudimentary emotions in trees, but it was extremely fleeting. Trees live in the immediacy of the moment, not in a place of confused emotions. In the very moment I felt an energy just vaguely reminiscent of tree emotion . . . it was gone. On reflection, I do not consider it an emotion. Trees have conscious intelligence and use it well, communicating from one tree to another on an energetic level that is instantaneous. Even my words — from one tree to another — are a misrepresentation. In Nature, all trees share the consciousness of One 'universal' tree, no matter what species. Some trees are truly ancient, and they do take on a very different energy compared with a tree that is a few hundred years younger. I have felt and experienced that ancient energy, but I have no words to describe it. The best I can come close to is touching a tree energy that is consciously connected to the stars: a tree that shares this with all trees as One. Such ancient trees are few today, for natural lifespans are decreasing as toxic pollution is increasing. Even as I do my best, my words are still inadequate to convey something which so few humans have ever truly experienced. We have no descriptive language for this.

I need to clarify a point here. Plants strongly respond to a loving human energy. A gardener who loves gardening will be very successful at it. Green thumb is the description for a plant lover . . . good energy. Trees respond to human love, even moss responds to human love. But, and here we hit a very big BUT . . . true Love is not an emotion. Love is the power of creation. However, where there is Love the emotions are high and fine, even though they are seldom actual Love. If you get into an aeroplane and go for a joy flight, when your emotions are high with the thrill, you are still not an aeroplane; you are still 'only' the passenger. In the same way, high emotions are the passenger of absolute Love. However, this is not the book to go into detail about this, except to say that true Love is the very deepest communication of great clarity, not only to all creatures, but also to all life. (Love and emotions are explained in greater detail in *From Illusion to Enlightenment.*)

Animals are different, but they do not fall under a single category of animals. Truly wild animals that have almost zero exposure to humans — and this is becoming rare — have emotions that briefly exist in the moment. They are felt and released very quickly. And let me reiterate that, in all my years of experience, these are *not human* emotions. Wild animals are focused in the moment of life; if any time were to be spent in emotional misery, the animal would quickly perish or be killed.

Please be aware that I am briefly touching on *emotions in animals,* not on animal intelligence. Whereas humans all fall within a certain range of the many and varied emotions, animals do not. The emotions of rats are very brief and rudimentary, while the emotions of elephants run far deeper and are much, much more complex and longer lasting.

Personally, I would throw away the idea of *human* emotions in *all* animals. Human emotions, intermixed and intermingled with our over-active and *undisciplined* imagination, are very convoluted. When people insist on inflicting their emotions onto trees and animals, they often create some seriously strange beliefs. Remember, animals do not have our imagination.

Animals that have a connection with people, such as farm animals and zoo animals, are definitely influenced by human emotions. They do not have human emotions, but they feel them as energy and are often confused by the complexity of this. Fear would be the greatest of the emotions that confuse and stress animals. As I have stated earlier, some animals will attack the low frequency of fear with amazing aggression, while others will shrink and cower from it. This behaviour is often seen in some dogs when they meet a stranger.

I have never owned a horse, nor do I ride, but a horse is very sensitive to human emotions. As a generalisation, if you get on a horse in an angry mood, you will have a rough ride. Get on the same horse with feelings of gratitude and love toward the horse, and the ride will be most enjoyable. Your emotions are energy, and energy is always communicating. Like it or not, you are in perpetual communication with every living thing around you. This never ends. Your thoughts and emotions are certainly yours, but you share them with the world! This steeply diminishes while you sleep, yet to a much lesser degree it continues.

What you communicate on an energetic level will determine your experience with any animal you encounter. If you are full of self-doubt, or have low self-worth, or are angry with yourself or someone else, you are communicating all this to an animal as a very threatening and confusing energy. They will react according to their own nature.

Finally, we have our pets.

Of all the animal kingdom, none are more exposed to human emotions than pets. There are many and varied animal stories about our pets that display an amazing amount of conscious intelligence. But I am writing about emotions. (Conscious intelligence in animals is another subject.) The emotions of pet owners have a huge effect on their pets. Less so on snakes and lizards and other reptiles, and far more so on dogs. Having said this, I need to add that snakes are very strongly affected by fear in people. However, people who keep snakes do so because they love the beautiful smooth critters, so the snakes get good energy and are considerably more docile — depending on the species of snake!

Cats have an independent streak that, to a degree, protects them from the full brunt of human emotions. Dogs seem to take it all in. Having been in a pet cat and a pet dog metaphysically and, expecting a difference, I was still very surprised by the degree of difference. I then tried the same with quite a number of pet cats and dogs, but the difference was always apparent. Cats *are* affected by our emotions and they do not particularly like it. It seems to threaten their independence, which is very much part of a cat's nature. This independence also varies in different cats of different species, but overall it is a fairly strong energy in them. I found that all the cats I was metaphysically within seemed able to withdraw from our emotions on an inner level, while still enjoying our caressing and stroking them. A few of the cats protected themselves by only allowing a fairly minimum, or limited, physical contact.

I have no hesitation in saying that a huge percentage of pet ailments are owner induced. Obviously, with the cost of pet care and surgery this is not deliberate. Ill health in pets is a thriving and profitable business. It is the result of the sometimes overwhelming *emotional needs* of the owner. Many pet owners have a toxic relationship with themselves. They then lavish all their affection on their pets that they, the owners, are not getting. Quite honestly, no pet can withstand this without fairly constant health problems.

Just as all our sickness and ill health is directly related to our emotions, so with our pets, they also suffer from our emotional imbalances. I have yet to meet a veterinarian who will actually tell the owner that they, the owner, are the pet's health problem, but I have spoken to many of them who are very aware of this. As one vet said to me, "If I was fully honest with all our pet owners I would be out of business!" Dogs are the most affected by this. Some loyal dogs quite literally soak up and absorb the anxieties, worries and fears of their owners. Under this constant influence they get sick, ageing quite rapidly.

It is an unfortunate fact that many pet owners have a poor relationship with themselves, meaning, a lack of self-Love. These people unknowingly rely and depend on the unconditional love of their pets. This particularly applies to the devotion that dogs can bestow on us. I will go as far as to say that if every person experienced absolute Love for themselves, there would be far fewer pets — owned and spoiled — and considerably more animal companions.

Without doubt, so many cat and dog owners look for the love from their pets that they cannot give to themselves. And it is okay. It is as it is. As we humans grow in consciousness, so our pets will grow and benefit with us.

Summary: Whether physical or metaphysical, our interactions with Nature will always be wide-ranging and different. We each experience life differently within our personal realities, and we each experience Nature differently. Please, do not chase validation. Once you get caught up in needing validation, you will never learn to trust yourself.

Let me remind you again that my words about the emotions of the plants and animals of Nature are no more than a brief overview. To do it justice it is a very deep subject that, for me, would have no purpose regarding your entering the secret world of Nature. If we reduced the need for left-brain understanding, and increased our right-brain ability to embrace the natural world, we would reap the full benefits of this. Wandering down the narrow lanes of mental and emotional speculation causes us to bypass our intended goal.

Chapter Eighteen

WHAT IS HOLISTIC INTUITION?

With regards to communicating with Nature, nothing is of greater value or more important for you than your intuition. For me, intuition is the voice of consciousness itself. All life is energy, and energy speaks to humanity through the language of intuition. What we call 'instinct' is more animalistic. Animals act on instinct, while we have the opportunity to act from intuition. We could look at the word as inner-tuition, *or inner teacher. It is sad that such a priceless gift as intuition has been dismissed by the intellect as unreliable. It is clear that when this happens, intelligence is absent.*

As far as I am concerned, intuition gets a bad rap in our left-brain dominant world. As a generalisation only, I have learned that women are more intuitive than men. However, this may be only because women are more inclined to trust their intuition, while men are far more pragmatic. But not all men. I am strongly intuitive, and my intuition has been the guiding factor of my life. Carolyn is also strongly intuitive. For better or worse, with most men it is the logical and reasoning brain that guides them!

With regards to communicating with Nature, nothing is of greater value or of more importance for you than your intuition. For me, intuition is the voice of consciousness itself. All life is energy, and energy speaks to humanity through the language of intuition. What we call 'instinct' is more animalistic. Animals act on instinct, while we have the opportunity to act from intuition. We could look at the word as *inner-tuition,* or inner teacher. It is sad that such a priceless gift as intuition has been dismissed by the intellect as unreliable. It is clear that when this happens, intelligence is absent.

Some people ask, what is intuition? Good question. Where does it come from, and what sparks it? Let us look at this.

In our heart we have seven groups of muscles. With a normal person, in everyday life, these groups of muscles are rather random in their movements; they are not at all coordinated. People's thoughts are mostly subconscious, frequently touching anger and leaping from deep anxiety to gusts of laughter and back within seconds. These scattered thoughts are always accompanied by our sub-emotions. Thoughts precede emotions. It is the emotional content of our thoughts that lift us one moment and plunge us down the next.

When, or if, you are more conscious of being conscious in the moment, more aware, and probably more spiritually focused, an amazing natural transformation takes place; the muscles of the heart become coherent. Their movements take on a coherency which greatly increases our heart energy. All this is well documented. HeartMath has a great deal of information on this. I experience this energy, so I know what it feels like. My heart coherency came from the natural evolution of my consciousness. I understand that there are techniques and exercises to induce heart coherency which are very effective, although I have never read about them or practiced them.

When the heart is coherent in its energy, a greater energy will flow from the heart to the brain. As this happens, a huge potential awaits, but it does depend on other factors. When, or if, you have developed a whole-brain way of living, this heart energy flows up to, and connects with the holistic brain. When this happened for me, I was aware of my brain energy changing, of new neural pathways opening up, and of a greater capacity within my brain. I am still learning how to use this greater capacity and its potential.

As the combination of coherent heart/holistic brain energy is now increased within this very holistic connection, so the energy reaches toward the pineal gland to further the human potential.

This can be a problem. In modern humanity, most people live in a way that has for a long time suppressed pineal growth and development. You will probably have to take my word for this, but in my metaphysical journeying I have visited people of the Palaeolithic period. Interestingly, they were far more sophisticated than is realised. They were also hugely more intuitive while being considerably less intellectual than we are. Personally, I witnessed more intelligence among them than I do in the actions of modern society, but intuition and intelligence go hand-in-hand. However, my metaphysical investigation also showed that their pineal glands, the size of a bean, were much bigger than ours of today. Our average pineal gland is the size of a grain of rice. A big difference!

At the time this shocked me.

I — and probably many others like me — have continued to develop the pineal. Being right-brain dominant means that the brain and the pineal are far more used and synchronised in their actions. As I earlier mentioned, I have followed my intuition all my life. Unrealised, this was developing the pineal gland. Let me give you an idea of how very different the Palaeolithic people were compared with modern society. A hunter in a clan might speak to the rest of the people: "I have seen into a valley that is a five-day journey from here. There are many forested hills and numerous valleys. In one of the valleys there is a herd of elk. I can lead us to them." With this said, and needing the food, the leather, and the bones, the clan prepare to walk the five days to the place that he has seen through the eyes of his intuition. Nobody challenges him. Nobody asks, "How can you possibly see five days away?" He is a hunter, and he has learned to far-see. They know this and they trust him completely with their lives.

Can you imagine this scenario in modern society?! "What makes you think you can see that far? Get real, man!" Or, "Wow, you have a drone that far away that you can control." Or, "If you think we are all going to walk that far on your say so, then you had better think again!"

One of the reasons of their superior pineal development was their self-reliance. Every person relied on the clan, and the clan relied upon every person. It was a continual and equal self-reliance for men and women. Today, we rely on the government, on the unemployment benefit, on the local council, on the shops, on the Internet, on so much that is external to us. Yes, we also rely on ourselves to earn the money to live, but that is about all. Okay, I could write far more about the reasons, but that is not the issue in this book.

I am writing about the pineal because *you need to develop it* if you have an intention to enter the secret world of Nature. The pineal gland *is* the third eye. It will open when it is stimulated and naturally developed. This is where you will be guided from. This is where Nature will speak to you, will instruct you on the right moves, will reveal herself to you. This is where the secrets of Nature are displayed and disclosed.

There is far more that happens within the body from the coherency of the heart, but that is not relevant for this book. What is relevant is the holistic heart/whole-brain/pineal connection. The so-called third eye is about inner seeing, not outer seeing. Two eyes are quite enough for that. We just need to use them more efficiently in the moment, rather than the all too often seen-it-all glance.

One of the vital factors of pineal growth is trust. This means that you are required to *trust your intuition*, not analyse and dismiss it. And in the dominant left-brain society of today, logic and reason are the guiding factors. Real trust is very, very uncommon. Trust is also hugely misunderstood. I could write a chapter on trust, but again, it is not appropriate for this book. You can read about trust in my book, *From Illusion to Enlightenment*. You will have to trust me on the necessity of developing trust by consciously using it. Remember, you cannot subconsciously trust! Trust can only be a fully conscious action.

Just as a word of caution, fluoride is the enemy of the pineal. Fluoride in your toothpaste should be avoided; there are many more natural ones. Avoid drinking water containing fluoride or chlorine. Make sure that it is *efficiently* filtered. Chlorine has a negative effect on your pineal, and chlorine is in nearly all household cleaners. It is also in personal tissues, toilet tissues and in tea bags, just to name a few. I could tell you much about the problems in human mental health brought about by our diminishing pineal, and none of it is good. Enough to reiterate that you will benefit in every way by stimulating and developing your pineal, along with balancing your brain.

Summary. I cannot over-state the need to develop your intuition. The physical functions of your pineal are basically the production of melatonin for sleep and serotonin for lifting your emotions, or moods.

Metaphysically, the pineal energy is the interface between the spiritual energy of a person and the spiritual energy of the universe. When the pineal energy fades, the sense of separation and isolation increases. This is causing huge mental health problems today that are misdiagnosed and mistreated because the medical people of today have an almost zero relationship with the holistic person and the holistic universe in which we live.

If you, however, wish to be a person who can interact with the secret world of Nature, then you have to be a person who is spiritually conscious of what is involved. Trust me, the pineal is *very powerfully* involved. Small the pineal gland may be, but metaphysically it is a powerhouse.

Chapter Nineteen

THE SPIRITS OF NATURE

I have encountered hundreds of nature spirits of forms and shapes I could never have imagined. You need to remember that we live in what could best be described as a restricted-reality zone. We are severely restricted in what we can actually see and hear. Unfortunately, this has become the world for most people, with a huge high wall around it. Not a good idea. The world of a greater reality is filled with many other Beings. We have vast numbers and types of elemental Beings; these are literally the elemental energies of the creation of the forerunners of all physical Nature.

As I have emphasised many times, we are limited to seeing less than one percent of the visual spectrum; similarly, we hear less than one percent of the audial spectrum. It beggars the mind regarding just what it is that we do not see or hear. To enter the secret spaces of Nature you, literally, are required to move beyond our everyday physical bandwidth into a higher spectrum of vision and sound ... in other words, a higher finer bandwidth.

Let me state very clearly that many people have hugely different experiences with, and of, the spirits of Nature. You should not listen to, or read, any one person and say, "Okay, this is how I do it. This is what I can expect. This is how it is." Some of the people who experience nature spirits teach their methods and techniques on how you may do this. I have no problem with this. I am just warning you that people are all very different, and just as there is no one single *diet* that works for everyone, equally there is no single *method* of entering into the realm of the nature spirits that works for everyone.

I have read a fair few books on other people's experiences with nature spirits, and while I can empathise with some, I find that none of them truly reflect my own experiences. This does not mean that I deny or doubt the authors. It means "To your own self, be true" . . . as Shakespeare would say. I had a friend, now deceased, who would walk a little way into the forests, and settling on a log or tree stump, he would see nature spirits very clearly with his inner eye. I am basically unable to do this, although I have on a few odd occasions. He was an artist, so he would make quick and very accurate sketches of them, eventually filling in the colour and details at home.

I very rarely see nature spirits or animal spirits with my inner eye while physical. I need to enter that realm/bandwidth, then I can both see them and interact with them. He was unable to do this. He was stuck in the physical all the time, even though he was able to see into their realm. If he wanted to see nature spirits of a certain type, this is what he saw. When I enter that realm, I never know quite what to expect . . . as it is mostly the unexpected that I see and experience.

I am explaining this so that you are aware of the need to accept your own experiences. Never compare yourself or your experiences with other people. We are each unique. Never criticise an experience that was a bit wobbly, a bit unclear, even a bit vague. It happens as it happens. For all of us who enter these realms, or even simply communicate with Nature, we have our 'off' days. The days when we need not have bothered! It is also interesting to note that the moon exerts a considerable influence on your interactions with Nature's realm, and on whether your efforts to connect may flow easily or are completely blocked.

Most gardeners are aware of the moon's influence on growth and timing when setting seedlings and sowing seeds. I am aware of it but I seldom follow it — sometimes to my detriment. But the moon's waxing and waning influence is very well documented regarding plant growth. As we all know, the tides of our worlds oceans and seas are caused by the phases of the moon. Plants are filled with sap/water, which also rises and falls under the moon's influence, although this is not visible to the naked eye. We also are physically over seventy percent water, so we too are far more affected by the moon than is realised. For example: the moon has a strong effect on women's menstruation and her accompanying moods. We are all affected. We do not have our words like 'lunacy' for no reason. This seems to be one of those cases where we have the knowledge of the lunar influence, but it does not apply to us!

Whether by day or night, the moon and the sun — and the stars — wield their influences on us, yet we are seldom aware of this. Astrologists are the exception to this, as they have made a study of the cosmic influence. I have learned that just as a physical Nature is affected by the stars, so also are the nature spirits. Just as I am unable to describe the stars influence on an everyday person, I am equally unable to describe how it influences the nature spirits. I only know that observation has taught me that on the not-so-good, 'wobbly' days of my inner connecting with Nature, I was sometimes aware of a slightly negating energy that affected me not only physically, but also metaphysically. And it also seemed to create a resistance toward me from within the nature spirits. This observation came more in hindsight, so I am unable to say whether the moon was waxing or waning at these times.

Having said this, I need to state that this was in my early years. My moods were more variable, my patience was much less, my attention could wander, and thoughts were a problem. Now, my focus into the metaphysical and moving into my Light body is very seldom affected by the phases of the moon or negatively influenced by the stars ... or me!

Having warned you not to compare your experiences with other people, and not to get caught up in right or wrong, or should or should not, I have one more warning to issue ... the mind. Then we will get right to the heart of this subject ... the nature spirits!

The mind ... ah, the mind! Not *your* mind or *my* mind, but *the* mind. I will keep this as brief as possible. Mind is universal. A person who says, "I can't make up my mind," is really saying, "I'm confused." You do not have a personal mind to make up, but you do have your personal connection with universal mind. And it is this personal connection that I wish to address.

To create a metaphor, you could compare mind with the bandwidths. There are the lower, heavy, human energies of mind, and there are the higher, finer, human energies of mind. Many people live their lives in the lower energies, and life is a struggle for them. Fewer people live in the higher, finer energies. Most people live somewhere in the space between lower heavy and higher finer. Thus they have visits to the lower heavier energy and visits to the higher finer energy. *To communicate with Nature, or to enter the realms of the Nature spirits, means that your connection with mind must be in the higher, finer energies during this process.*

Okay, I realise that this is a rather different way of describing mind, but I do not wish to get involved with the complexities and beliefs that our current academic world has regarding mind. I experience mind in a different way. It works very powerfully for me and for those who actually comprehend what I am teaching. A concept of what I am saying/ writing does not work!

Okay ... the spirits of Nature.

We probably have Walt Disney to thank for the deeply imprinted, mostly beautiful technicolour images of fairy and elf spirits of Nature. I, too, was in awe of the Disney movie, Fantasia. It is not easy to surrender those images. You will notice that all, or most, of our images of the nature spirits are in our own image — rather human looking, even if tiny.

Let me share an experience of many years ago when I first met one of this vast realm of nature spirits. As I write about this, I feel a degree of mild embarrassment at my level of naivety. But ... I was as I was!

I was sitting on a large tree stump on top of a hill. The hill was powerful in energy, that was obvious even to me! The stump was big enough for me to sit cross-legged, a big error! I wanted to meet with a nature spirit, so I sat in meditation for maybe an hour, and nothing was happening. By this stage my feet had died on me, all that was left was pins and needles. And flies, and a few mosquitoes! I was so acutely uncomfortable that I wanted to bring it all to an end ... but I was also stubborn.

Just as I was about to give in, I suddenly noticed I was inner-seeing an elf standing very close to me. He was almost one metre tall — this shocked me — and was dressed in a one piece, skin-tight fitting garment that was a grass green in colour. He was looking at me in a very patient but quizzical manner.

"Oh," I gasped. "Oh ... er, hello."

He greeted me with a nod of his head and a smile.

I was completely flummoxed. Now what was I supposed to do?

"Er ... can I ask you a question?"

Of course, he replied.

Of all the cosmic questions of depth and meaning I could have asked! I am almost cringing as I write the truth.

"Er ... how do you put your cloths on?" I asked. "There is no zip, no neckline, no join anywhere. Everything looks like your skin, except it's a material of some sort. How could you possible get into it?"

The elf looked at me pityingly.

I do not get into it. This is how I am. Do you not like me?

"Oh, I like you well enough, but it doesn't make sense. How can you wear clothes that are you? Clothes are separate."

Instantly, standing in the same place was a faun. No sign of an elf, or of any clothes!

Do you prefer this?

Now I was completely confused. The faun was about the same height as the elf, but very different. He had a boy's body and face, the legs and feet of a kid — a young goat — with short shaggy fur on the kid parts and a type of furry skin on the boy parts. He also had a pair of tiny horns, one on each side of his outer forehead.

"Where did *you* come from?" I gasped.

With a mild sigh, the faun vanished and a ball of Light about the size of a golf ball floated in front of me.

Make up your mind. Which is easiest for you to relate to. All these are me. Form is variable, so I will assume your choice.

I knew that I could best relate to the elf. Even before I spoke the words to him, the elf reappeared.

And so my first conversation with a nature spirit continued.

The point I am making is that nature spirits generally take the form that is most familiar in the mind of the person they are interacting with. For many centuries our fairy stories have gradually cemented certain forms and figures into the human psyche, thus we see tiny faeries, elves and the more familiar forms that we have been programmed with. In Ireland people tend to see the familiar Leprechauns, while in some of the Nordic countries it is Trolls. Of course, most people do not believe in such nonsense and see none of this.

I have encountered hundreds of nature spirits in forms and shapes I could never have imagined. You need to remember that we live in what could best be described as a restricted-reality zone. We are severely restricted in what we can actually see and hear. Unfortunately, this has become the world for most people, with a huge high wall around it. Not a good idea. The world of a greater reality is filled with many other Beings. We have vast numbers and types of elemental Beings; these are literally the elemental energies of the creation of the forerunners of all physical Nature.

Trees did not just become trees via the process of evolution. By looking and evaluating only from a physical reality, science has to make our physical evolution fit all the answers to the many questions that are presented by life. And because science says this is the way it is, those who live in the restricted reality world accept and believe . . . and they are the huge majority. Luckily there are always other, more open maverick academics and scientists who continually push against the limits of accepted beliefs.

Elementals are the predecessor energy of the physical forms that will then continue to physically and spiritually evolve. Even humanity has its elemental energy of each period in our long evolution of consciousness. Remember, all evolution is the evolution of consciousness seeking to explore shapes and forms that will lead to an even more efficient evolution. Nature is brilliant! If you metaphysically explore a tree, you will encounter its elemental energy in various different forms. I have found several types in the roots of trees, in the trunk of the tree, and in its many branches. These elementals can be described as countless, they are so hugely numerous. Be aware that elementals and nature spirits are basically the same, although the true forerunner elementals are only involved when new species are emerging.

When the sun shines on the leaves of a tree, it is the millions of tiny nature spirits within each leaf that — using my term — 'stitch' the sun energy deeply into the leaves. Other types of nature spirits take that sun energy of illumination through the leaves into the stem, and on into the twigs and the slender branches and down through the thicker branches to the main trunk. At the trunk, another type of nature spirits take the sun illumination on down the trunk in such vast numbers it is almost like a flowing waterfall of the suns illumination.

When this flowing energy meets the huge root structure, so it flows into the widespread feeder roots carried by yet another type of nature spirit. In the deep anchor roots there is another type taking the energy downward. Into the roots that go deepest, mining the deep soil profile for its mineral content, yet another type of nature spirit prevails. Finally, when the roots of the deep mining roots are no thicker than a human hair and writhing with energy, so the illumination of the sun energy is carried kilometres deep into the subsoil. The Earth knows the sun in a way that humanity can never imagine. And all this is happening in every moment of the trees long life.

No microscope can detect or measure any of this. None of it is three-dimensional. So in the restricted world, my description of a growing tree is a *fairy story* . . . beyond belief!

When your connection with mind is high and fine, so you will encounter stunningly beautiful and powerful nature spirits. These are usually involved in the various more complex expressions of Nature. A perfect example of this are the forest devas. A more evolved deva oversees the evolution of a whole forest, while a less evolved deva will oversee the evolution of a single plant or tree species. In all this, there is a powerful hierarchy, but there is absolutely no lesser or greater involved.

In the trunks of some older trees, you may find a dryad. This is a single species type of deva. Interestingly, just as we can get attached to a rather magnificent home to such an extent that we may well reincarnate back to it for several lifetimes — not a good idea — so this can occasionally happen to a tree dryad. I have encountered tree dryads that are free-moving from one tree to another, and I have come across those that became attached to a tree, and are stuck within it until the tree eventually dies. Of course, there is no linear time in this metaphysical reality, so they are unaware of time passing. Indeed, in their reality time does not pass by!

Some of the overall forest devas are vast, with their energy reaching many kilometres into the sky. Some writers and intuitives attempt to give even these a human-like shape, but in my experiences this is not so. They are Beings of Light just as we are, but without our accompanying physical form. Entering the secret world of Nature reveals far more than anyone can conceptually grasp. There needs to be a huge surrender in the person. They need to accept that they are the merest child in this new and vast reality world. Sure, the human child is powerful in their own restricted world, but as truly metaphysical Beings, we are designed for the greater reality world. Here true humility is our greatest power. True humility is about recognising our true greatness, not cringing as a lesser person under the whip of the ego.

Summary: If or when you enter the secret world of Nature, you will eventually encounter nature spirits. Please, do not get a fixed and rigid idea or theory of what these may, or should, look like. I shared my first encounter so you will realise just how limited I was. I was unable to enter the realm of nature spirits that time, and for a fair few years after that. I seldom encountered an elf again that was as tall as that one, although it has been my experience that elves which interact with people on a regular basis are considerably bigger and more vocal than their Nature focused counterparts.

If Nature opens her secret world to you, enter gracefully and gratefully. Remember, your energy is continually communicating with all Nature, you cannot contain secret desires or deceits, all is shared and known. You will never be judged or condemned as in our human world, but your energy field will determine your experience. At least, this has always been the way it is for me. I like to keep my energy pure and simple.

Chapter Twenty

DELUSIONS — WEEDS — OCEANS

When people meditate they are allowing their brain to find the peace and quiet of their alpha brain rhythm. Questions cease. Worries are stilled. Anxiety released, or put on the back-burner. On all the inner levels of energy, they relax; metaphysically and physically. Most people need this on a daily basis, but only the few have the self-discipline to do it. I guess most people have never even considered it! If a student was to cease 'cramming' just before an important examination, and meditate for an hour, they would be in their top form. This would be intelligent!

On Facebook, I invited and received a lot questions for this book. Many of them are not usable because they were so intellectually left-brain, they were not applicable in a book of this type. As I have already stated many times, Nature is not an intellectual expression of energy; it is metaphysical first and foremost, yet also expressing through physical form. There are many books on Nature that are very intellectual; indeed, most of them are, so these will be the books for the people who look for a mental answer to their mental questions.

I write from my heart, from my experience and from my intuitive connection with all life. For me, this *is* the place of life — the movement in the moment. It is accessible to all, but it is only the few that avail themselves of this great gift.

A very common question: "How can I be sure that I am not deluding myself?" I smile at this, because the simple fact is that you are deluding yourself each and every day of your life. The very question indicates that you live so immersed in the illusion that its delusions completely evade you. Please do not be offended by my forthright reply; it is not personal. I just want you to see the question for what it is. What you are afraid of is actually more delusions within your many delusions in the illusion!

I am compelled to repeat myself: you cannot have this deep relationship with a secret Nature and remain the person you are now. You cannot Change and remain the same. You are required to *trust yourself* to a degree that you have never even contemplated. When they were children, many people had a quite deep and remarkable relationship with Nature. This was based in their openness, their lack of guile, their innocence. Their brain was still in its alpha mode, with its beta aspect not yet dominant. Once our education system begins to bring our beta rhythm to the fore, over-developing it, then all that is natural to us is compelled to recede. The intellect and its stupid cleverness takes over.

This is where I was very blessed. As a right-brain dominant child, our education system was so totally foreign to me that I rebelled. Hence, bottom of the class all the time. It was not a good experience, and I do not in any way recommend it, but I do suggest that you see the limits and pitfalls within our intellectual dominance of today. Balance your studies with meditation.

When people meditate they are allowing their brain to find the peace and quiet of their alpha brain rhythm. Questions cease. Worries are stilled. Anxiety released, or put on the back-burner. On all the inner levels of energy, they relax — metaphysically and physically. Most people need this on a daily basis, but only the few have the self-discipline to do it. I guess *most* people have never even considered it! If a student was to cease 'cramming' just before an important examination, and meditate for an hour, they would be in their top form. This would be *intelligent!*

Meditation before attempting to communicate with Nature would relax you, helping you past the doubts and fears of if you are being delusional. It would not take long before you would develop the trust in yourself to not need to do this first.

A similar question to the above is, 'how do I tell the difference between true communication and imagination?' What is true communication? Consider two people talking 'at' each other, with neither of them listening; is this true communication? I do not think so. Much of our human communication is quite dysfunctional. Two people shouting at each other, or arguing with each other, or even talking quietly to each other, yet attached to their own agenda. Seriously, a dog conveys more in its pee-mail than a person does in their email. And the dog is far more honest. What you smell is who I am. But what you read in an email about a person is often no more than the way you are being steered to believe and think!

As for imagination, if you are not using your receptive, non-attached and open imagination in your communication with Nature, then you are unable to receive. You could well describe your imagination as the antenna of deeper communication. Of course you are using your intuition, but this is connected to your imagination. We are holistic Beings, not a composite of separate parts! You are required to trust. Trust is holistic. There is no such thing as intellectual trust. You cannot partly trust, or sometimes trust. Trust is an energy that transforms your whole life. Real trust is so rare that people only have an intellectual understanding of the meaning of the word ... yet this is not trust! When you have complete trust in self, all questions fall by the wayside. And the only way to gain it is by fully trusting yourself in each and every moment of your life.

I am asked about weeds. 'How should I deal with them? Should I talk to them and ask them to go away? Is it okay to rip them out of the ground? Isn't such action cruel and thoughtless? Why do they keep growing back?'

First of all, what is a weed? There is no such thing as a weed plant. A weed is any plant in the wrong place at the wrong time. Some of the most beautiful flowering trees and garden plants in a cool temperate climate can become a serious weed in a sub-tropical climate. If you have bare land, it will soon become covered with what we call weeds. But those weeds are not just any random plants. They are mostly plants that, in the long term, will be of the greatest benefit to the soil. If you burn some garden rubbish on a regular basis in a part of the garden, quite often the first plant that will appear in the ashes will be thistles. I consider thistles as the *forgiveness* of Nature. Farmers hate them, and quite a few cooler climate gardeners.

When I was a dairy farmer in Tasmania, there was a seven-strand barbed-wire fence between my land and my neighbour's. He kept sheep on his pastures and it was constantly overgrazed. Overgrazing is the biggest crime in being a pastoralist. This went on year after year. On my side of the fence my cows were moved regularly, with the minimum of overgrazing. When you are in a drought, overgrazing is almost un-avoidable.

On his side of the fence, his land was covered in Scotch thistles, tall, thick and dense, and getting worse every year. The prevailing wind carried the floating seed from his thistles all over my large paddock alongside his.

One day, Reggie, the sheep farmer, asked me how it was that his thistle seed did not grow on my side of the fence. It made no sense. On my side of the fence I might get a scattering of maybe a hundred thistle plants over all the paddock, on his side hundreds of thousands. He could not understand.

So I told him. I explained that as he overgrazed his land every year, so he was driving down the pH of his soil. Then I had to explain pH! The lower the pH, the more acidic his soil. The more acidic his soil, the sicker it became. Thistles cannot be grazed by sheep or cattle, so they thrive. The roots plunge deep into the soil, bringing calcium into the plant via a variety of mineral transmutations. It was calcium and mag-nesium that was so lacking in his soil. When the older thistles die down each winter, so they release these vital minerals into the soil.

On my side of the fence, I was an organic farmer. Basically this meant that I did everything to encourage the proliferation of earth-worms and organic life in the soil. Under this influence the pH of my land was rising. At the time Reggie's soil was 4.5 pH; mine had risen to a pH of 5.9. Without going into all the details, the difference is huge. Reggie's acidic soil was the pH trigger that caused the germination of his thistle seeds. On my side of the fence, my soil pH did not trigger their germination. Nature knows exactly what is needed to bring any soil toward a greater fertility. We mostly call them weeds!

In an average lawn, the most persistent weeds are those that hold the minerals that are most lacking in that soil. Replace that mineral nutrient and the weeds will begin to recede. So it is with daisies, buttercups and so on. Moss in a lawn denotes a lack of oxygen in the soil, and excessive moisture. It needs its drainage improved.

Seriously, do not put human emotions onto weeds. It is okay to rip them out of the ground. As soon as your intent to do this is formed, they know. And they do not judge you or condemn you. This is human behaviour, not Nature's. Most people are cruel in their thoughts about themselves; this does serious damage!

I smile at asking weeds to go away. I tried to talk my acres of wild blackberries away on that farm, and it never worked. Finally I had to accept that what I wanted was irrelevant to Nature. The blackberries stayed, and I began to use toxic weedkillers on them. That is another story in itself! So, understand why the weeds are in your garden. Have the soil tested at a garden centre and do your best to balance the soil with all its needed mineral nutrients. This usually works.

I was asked about why people so enjoy the ocean. The question was not about water sports, surfing and the like; it was about our fascination with the sea. I remember as a kid, the sea at Hunstanton on the east coast of England was an absolute treat. And it was the sea, not the tedious journey. Much of this is to do with our compatibility with the ocean. Sure, we cannot breathe in water, but our tears and our lymphatic fluids — which are ten times the amount of our blood — are very similar in salt and water to the great oceans. In many ways we are a tiny ocean contained in physical bodies. For me, this attraction is a polarity thing. We need to polarise our energy on a regular basis with the Earth and the ocean. Living in cities full of concrete, in high-rise buildings disconnected from the Earth, and breathing in far too much city pollution every day all creates a serious imbalance for the wellbeing of our physical and metaphysical bodies.

Most people crowd into the city parks on any sunny weekend. The sun energy is needed by our body, even if we do think we just want a tan. The energy field of our body is positive, needing the negative energies of Nature, via the ocean and the Earth, to bring about balance. As you well know, this is not about positive good and negative bad; it is about the polarisation of our energy in a similar manner to a battery. A lack of this polarisation leads toward our extremes of behaviour that are becoming so prevalent in the cities: increased aggression, anger, road rage and severe drinking violence.

Many people have dreams that feature oceans, lakes or rivers. Many different meanings and interpretations are put to these, but I often think that the most simple explanation is often the most accurate. They either represent emotional turmoil or serenity — think about this! — or they are prompting us to once again get our polarisation fix.

Summary: Our fear of being delusional is misplaced. To enter the secret realms of Nature, you are required to go into a space/place that you not only do not intellectually understand, but you never truly will. But you can experience it.

Weeds are Nature's way of balancing the deficiencies of the soil. If you pull them out or hoe them away, it is okay. But then go the next step and balance the soil with its required nutrients and minerals.

Our oceans need to be respected, not filled with plastic. Of the two hundred, sixty million tons of plastic the world produces each year, about *ten percent* ends up in the oceans. At the time of writing this book, the Great Plastic Patch in the Pacific Ocean between the coasts of California and Hawaii is twice the size of Texas, USA. This unnatural blight in our oceans is to our great shame. It highlights the severity of our disconnection from Nature.

Chapter Twenty-One

QUESTIONS, QUESTIONS, QUESTIONS!

I have very clearly outlined many of the skills that need to be mastered. None of them are easy, yet all of them are simple. Each and every practice I have set before you is for your growth as a spiritual Being. You cannot be the person asking these questions and also be the person who enters the secret world of Nature. You cannot remain in prison and roam free. I know a man on death row in an American prison who, despite his physical body being imprisoned, has made such a quantum leap in consciousness that he is actually experiencing soul freedom. Nobody can imprison the soul that he is. He may not yet know it, but in his state of consciousness he could enter the secret world of Nature while his body remains imprisoned. It will not be too long before he reads this!

Below I offer an example of one person's response to my request for questions. There is no criticism implied, but this amount and flow of questions denotes a very dominant, left-brain approach to life. This is seen as normal even though it is not natural. Whereas this works in daily life, it does not work within a metaphysical Nature. As I address these questions, despite how I word my answers, they are to every reader, not just to the person who will recognise their questions. I am using them because they are very relevant to the greater picture. Some of these questions might appear to have nothing to do with Nature, but they do relate to the consciousness of entering that secret kingdom.

~ *Does the possibility of "stepping between" depend on my state of consciousness? Can anyone do it and right now? What do I have to master or know how to do it?*

~ *Does everyone have a spiritual guide? How do I find him or her? Is it enough to ask for contact internally? And how do I recognise him? Are there charlatans in metaphysics?*

~ *Is metaphysical journeying comparable to an out-of-body experience? Are you completely there with all your senses, or just in thought?*

~ *Does it have to be in meditation? Is it possible to do it while going for a walk?*

~ *In which areas or levels does the metaphysical divide? Is it like in shamanism? Lower, middle and upper world? Or is everything an area?*

~ *Can one be occupied by negative energies or Beings? If so, what can you do? Personally, I do not believe it, but since I have out-of-body experiences, many ask me about this in the Internet forums.*

~ *I suppose self-love is the best protection?*

Beginning at the top, I will briefly look at each question, hoping that this will help many of you who only asked a few. This should also cover many unasked questions. The questions will be italicised to avoid any confusion.

Does the possibility of 'stepping between' depend on my state of consciousness?

This question refers to one of my books on metaphysical journeying, *Stepping . . . Between . . . Realities.* Yes, this is absolutely about your state of consciousness. As I have already said, entering the inner realms of Nature is entirely about your state of consciousness. The higher you raise your state of consciousness, the easier it will be to cross over from the mundane to the magnificent — the bandwidth of a greater reality. This is what some of my earlier books are about: my experiences in other realities.

Can anyone do it, right now?

Everyone has the potential within them, but the probability of 'anyone' doing it, right now, is practically zero. I get a deep feeling of impatience in this person . . . and that's okay, but it will very much get in the way of their potential. The journey — in just this lifetime — I have undertaken to be the person I am today has lasted for over fifty years. As my journey progresses, so my potential expands exponentially. There is no quick fix for metaphysical journeying, or for any other true spiritual path. If it is not worth your time and dedication, then forget it and continue in the illusion game.

People sometimes tell me that they would like to have my state of inner consciousness. I usually ask them if they would like to experience all that I have experienced to reach my current state of consciousness. They quickly say, "No." Many of them know that my path was one of pain and suffering. I have done both . . . abundantly! This is why I teach people why and how to choose Love! For me, it is very, very important that I continue to grow in the consciousness of Love. Love knows nothing of impatience. On the contrary, Love is about infinite patience — with self and all others.

What do I have to master, or know how, to do it?

This whole book addresses that question. I have very clearly outlined the skills that need to be mastered. None of them are easy, yet all of them are simple. Each and every practice I have set before you is for your growth as a spiritual Being. You cannot be the person asking these questions and also be the person who enters the secret world of Nature. You cannot remain in your prison and roam free. I know a man on death row in an American prison who, despite his physical body being imprisoned, has made such a quantum leap in consciousness that he is actually experiencing soul freedom. Nobody can imprison the soul that he is. He may not yet know it, but in his state of consciousness he could enter the secret world of Nature while his body remains imprisoned. It will not be long before he reads this!

Does everyone have a spiritual guide?

Yes, everyone has a soul guide. Your soul guide has been with you ever since the soul you are began your first experience of being human. You are not a human soul; you are an infinite, limitless soul having a human experience. Very different. While you, in the physical body, experience linear time, probably often getting bored and/or frustrated during certain periods of your life, your metaphysical soul guide lives in time-lessness. No time passing, no boredom and no frustration. Considering many of the incarnating people that they accompany and guide, maybe this is just as well!

How do I find him or her? Is it enough to ask for contact inter-nally? And how do I recognise him or her?

Hmm . . . I wonder if you have a real soul-longing for this connection, or if it is just more fodder to stimulate the intellect? Before you look for or find your soul guide, you need to truly connect with yourself. You need to know who you are as a Being. You need to have a soul connection with Self. You are a normal physical identity-self, and you are a metaphysical soul-Self. People are very familiar with the perso-na-identity-self, but very much less so with their soul-Self. Ask yourself, which comes first in your life? The soul-Self whom you truly are, or the persona-identity-self you believe yourself to be?

You do not ask for contact as though you are going to collect another Facebook friend; you share the deep longing in your heart/soul to once again be connected. We spend very little time in our physical incarna-tions, yet we spend an enormous amount of so-called time — which is not actually linear time at all — metaphysically between incarnations. Your soul guide knows the soul you are a thousand times better than you do while physically incarnate. This suggests that your soul guide knows you now, in this moment, and knows your true intent. When 'you' are truly ready, you will find yourself being contacted. However, to feel this you are required to be conscious . . . not subconscious.

If your soul guide is metaphysically with you, then you cannot fail to recognise the soul connection — when, and only when, you are ready for that inner awareness. If they are physically in your life — this happens — it is not so easy to know who they are. It may be a grandchild, a friend, even someone who gives you a hard time. However, as you become ready via your growth in consciousness, and you trust yourself, you will intuitively know.

Are there charlatans in metaphysics?

There are certainly plenty of charlatans in everyday life, many of them are politicians and purported world leaders, but I question your question. Every charlatan has a metaphysical body, we all do, but no one develops spiritual growth through deception or devious means. I am at loss to your meaning. All I can say is that in all my many metaphysical journeys I have never met a so-called charlatan.

To consciously enter into a greater reality you have to *grow* in consciousness, you cannot *regress* into a higher realm. So how could there be charlatans? All charlatans are definitely earthbound. Most probably there are charlatans who make claims of what they can metaphysically do. We are very much in a time of false prophets. Never give your power to anyone; not even the greatest of spiritual teachers; not anyone. I often experience a person or people inadvertently attempting to give me their power, but I never take it. Never. People who attend my Intensives are very aware of this.

Is metaphysical journeying comparable to an out-of-body experience? Are you completely there with all your senses, or just in thought?

An out-of-body experience only takes place while you are sleeping. This happens to everybody. The difference is being *conscious* of your out-of-body experience and remembering it. This is, or was, generally known as astral travel, simply because that is exactly what it is! To astral travel you must have your body asleep: there are exceptions to this, but they are very few.

With my metaphysical journeying I am very much awake in my

physical body. Most people *believe* they are a physical person, so they identify strongly with the body. I know that I am a metaphysical Being — we all are — so I identify more with my Light-body. To journey I focus deeply into my Light-body, letting go of thoughts — and wants — and all such distractions. I allow my sense of self as Light to move away from the physical body. I *know* I am not imprisoned. In many ways, what people do at night with the body asleep, I have learned to do with the body awake. The astral realms we journey in are the same, but I have a far greater awareness and comprehension of who I am, where I am, and where I am going . . . and usually, with whom!

Regarding being there with all my senses . . . yes, I am. In some ways, more so than when awake. My sense of perception, or discernment, in my Light-body is far greater than in my physical body. When we are physical, it is very rare for us to holistically experience life. We mostly use the five, basic, bodily senses. When I am metaphysical, I am holistically present. For me to attempt to describe this in words is a bit like you explaining colour to a blind person.

Does metaphysical journeying have to be in meditation? Is it possible to do it while going for a walk?

This depends very much on the person involved. Most people find that a meditative state of consciousness is very helpful. Certainly you have to be free of worry and anxiety, of wants and desires, of our many expectations and worldly, ego-based attachments . . . so yes, a meditative state is a good way to go. Do I do this? No, I do not. I consider that my whole day is lived in a light meditative state of consciousness. There are moments I drop out of this, but they do not last.

Is it possible to metaphysically journey while walking? Yes, it is possible. I have done it, but having walked unseeing into a tree, I seldom do so now. Outside walking tends to invite a lot of distractions. I prefer to be comfortable, sitting in my study.

In which areas or levels does the metaphysical divide? Is it like in shamanism? Lower, middle and upper world? Or is everything an area?

Hmm . . . divide or division is entirely an intellectual concept. It works in mathematics, but nothing truly divides in a holistic reality. However, I concede that division *appears* to be real in a world where people believe in separation. Having never had anything to do with shamanism at all, I cannot answer that. Certainly it is the same astral reality that we experience, although even the astral world has its own bandwidths. I have no intention of attempting to explain that! Once again: the higher your state of consciousness as you explore the astral realms of Nature's secret world, the deeper will be your experiences, and the wider the gate to mystical reality swings open.

Trust me on this; there is nothing that your intellect can grab hold of and understand in the greater reality of eternity.

Can one be occupied by negative energies or beings? If so, what can you do? Personally, I do not believe it, but since I have out of body experiences many ask in the Internet forums. I suppose self-love is the best protection?

For a person who apparently has out-of-body experiences, they are poorly informed on their subject. Yes, you can certainly have a negative entity enter your body, and they can be very difficult to dislodge. And if not removed or dislodged, they will end your physical life prematurely. I have encountered a fair number of people who obviously carry an entity. Many alcoholics are actually plunged into the lower astral when they are inebriated. This is a seriously dangerous practice. It is almost as easy to pick up an entity this way as it is to pick up fleas from a stray dog. I find it disturbing that this person shares their out-of-body experiences on the Internet forums, but appears to know so little about the subject. No wonder I never get involved in these forums!

What can you do to get rid of them? First and foremost, negative entities are attracted to a lower state of consciousness. Anger, hate, rage, critical, blaming, judging, holding grievances, etc., are common traits in people. All this takes a person into a lower state of consciousness. Can you experience an out-of-body experience like this? Yes, you can. In the natural state of sleep lower astral experiences come across as nightmares. In an out-of-body experience you can have some very bad encounters. Not a good idea. However, you *cannot* metaphysically journey with this low energy as your baseline. No way!

The flippant statement, *I suppose self-love is the best protection* speaks to me of a person who is totally devoid of truly *experiencing* self-Love. I have no hesitation whatsoever in stating that unconditional self-Love is the most rare of all human experiences on this planet today. You cannot Love yourself or anyone subconsciously, and over ninety percent of humanity lives subconsciously. When you are unconditionally Loving, self protection, or the perceived need of defence is an invalid concept. You are the world!

Okay . . . enough of this person's questions.

This question creates a good summary.

How do I get out of my own way?

Summary: First, ask yourself, what is it that gets in your own way? For most people it is quite a long list: fear of the unknown, mind chatter, self-doubt, anxiety. Will I get stuck? Is it dangerous? How do I know if it is real? The list goes on and on. All of this is lower consciousness stuff. It is not wrong or bad, there is no criticism implied, it just does not work for you. Actually it does not work in your daily life, so it certainly will not work if you wish to enter the secret world of Nature. Why is it a so-called secret? It is not, but it is an exploration that very few people are yet ready to undertake. An old quote is quite astute: 'Out of sight, out of mind.' With the greater metaphysical reality being on a higher bandwidth, then it is certainly out of the sight and out of the mind of the otherwise engaged masses.

You need to take your thoughts out of the way by practicing inner silence. If you are *fully trusting* yourself, there is no fear, no self-doubt, no anxiety. When you know the *real self*, there will be no question: 'Is it real?'

Remember, you were born for this; it is your birthright as a metaphysical Being. I urge you to claim that birthright.

Chapter Twenty-Two

MORE QUESTIONS ANSWERED

Once, many years ago when I lived in Tasmania, I visited a forest that had been plundered by the loggers of the wood chip industry. It was a scene of devastation, the rape and ruin of a forest, a desecration of natural beauty. I sat on a tree stump as I looked around me, and I wept. As my rather shocked emotions slowly stabilised, and I wiped the tears from my eyes, very slowly emerging into my inner eye I saw that the whole forest was standing, every tree, every plant, all growing in pristine metaphysical perfection.

I am engaging in more questions because these bring out aspects of Nature that I might have not even considered. Equally, one person's question is many people's question. I have lightly edited the questions, removing all that is irrelevant and chatty, and correcting the English. Many of the questions come from all over Europe.

An insightful question:

I learned by reading your books that the big connection to Nature was listening ... without thoughts .... just sitting and being with and listening. Also just talking to trees, touching leaves, talking to the river ... and then being quiet, listening without thoughts. So my question is this: is it more about a 'relaxing' than a 'doing'? Is it more about a 'listening' than 'asking' questions? Is it more about 'allowing' Nature to unfold itself?

This person is very perceptive. A big Yes, to all the questions. Yes, it is far more about *relaxing* than doing. There is nothing to 'do'. We have over-developed a 'doing to' consciousness. We are *doing to*, but seldom ever *being with*, while doing to. We are 'doing to' while lost in a whirlwind of crazy thoughts. '*Doing to' while 'being with' is the art of living*. It is the art of connecting with Nature on deeper levels. What we are 'doing' is seeking connection with Nature; but we need to be with the moment for this to happen. Remember, Nature is never outside the moment, and we are so rarely in it.

Yes, of course we need to spend more time in Nature *listening*, rather than in asking questions. We cannot question and be fully in the moment! People are so full of questions. We have been brainwashed to believe that progress is made by asking questions. Intellectual progress, maybe, but the progress of conscious intelligence, no. Intelligence is aligned with being conscious, not subconscious. This is the realm of the intellect, and again, Nature is not an intellectual expression.

Yes, it is more about *allowing* than seeking. The art of life is to allow, not to force, or manipulate, or make happen. When you focus on developing your consciousness, everything happens in perfect timing. Allowing is a power. It is a power inherent within knowing. I live my life allowing life to happen. I allow life to roll the dice . . . and I play accordingly.

Some people ask me, "Why are you not world famous?" I reply, "If I was world famous, it would give me nothing spiritually more than I have now. If being world famous is within the scheme of my life, so be it. I will accept it."

An energetic question:

Many years ago, the lane I walked towards my work was lined with old eucalyptus trees. On my way home, I saw that one of the oldest trees had been cut down. My heart sank and I went to the stump and touched the raw cut. The energy was amazing. I can still remember the feeling of it today. On the way to work the next day I touched it again — but the energy had gone.

Another time in Mexico some spear fishermen had killed a big fish — I asked if I could look at it — so I could touch it. And again, the energy I felt was like the tree shared. It was amazing! What do Nature Beings feel about or sense as physical form comes to an end? How do they react to illness or bad conditions in Nature?

We are mental and emotional Beings, thus we develop strong opinions about good and bad and right and wrong, should and should not, etc. The devas and spirits of Nature do not have strong mental and emotional expressions. Certainly they perceive most people as amazingly destructive to themselves. People never seem to realise that mental and emotional destruction is turned inwards, so people destroy themselves: sickness, so-called accidents, diseases, and the like. It is all self-created.

We believe that we are physical form, but the Nature Beings are under no such delusion. They *know* that the form is a physical reflection from a greater metaphysical reality; it is all about bandwidths! To these Nature Beings, everything of a physical Nature is short-lived and transient. Change is a permanent expression of Nature, it is the nature of growth. This obviously indicates that they have no relationship with what we term as illness or bad conditions. In Nature, it is as it is.

A peculiar question:

> *How peculiar does an experience need to be in order to be termed as metaphysical travel in the world of Nature? When I simply listen to the energy of love and am obviously guided by it, can I say I am traveling with my feet in the secret world of an intimate Nature, despite the physical circumstances?*

What does peculiar have to do with anything? If you listen to the energy you call Love, and it guides you . . . what more do you want? What do you need explained? Are you attached to phenomena? It seems to me that you, like so many other people, need to have the bells and whistles of phenomena accompany your endeavours for it to be real or acceptable. Only you know your experience. You have a choice: stumbling doubt, or easy acceptance. I took the stumbling doubt path for a few years; you do not need to. Just accept your experience for the way it

167

is, and as it is. Do not compare. Do not seek for others to tell you if it is real or false. Trust in yourself. As you develop, your inner experiences will also grow and develop. Would you expect a child to start running before it has learned to walk?

A problematic question:

> *My problem is that as soon as I get into a routine while trying to learn or to exercise something on the spiritual level, it becomes repetitive and intellectual and stays on the surface. It's just words in my head. That's why I try to just go with the flow and practice what pops up when it pops up, and this works really well. However, communication with Nature, not just my cats and bird, but the plants and wild birds in my garden, the Earth and so on, is something I am longing for. How can I be sure I get communication? How can I know it is not my imagination, but what was communicated with me? How do I do that? Where is my problem?*

I agree with you. A routine approach or a repetitive technique does become words in the mind, a game in the intellect. So you found the answer to this by being spontaneous. When something just pops up and engages you, go with the flow. You are right on track . . . so far!

Okay, the intellect is now questioning the authenticity of your hoped-for communication with Nature. It asks many distracting and disturbing questions, like, is it imagination? Let us be very clear about this. While you allow your intellect to question and interrogate your inner experiences of communication, you will never — repeat, never — get acceptance. Your left-brain cannot communicate with Nature, so how do you expect it to accept it? It will always question and ridicule. Your right-brain or whole-brain will not have these doubts and questions, only the dominant left-brain. Left-brain dominance is your problem, not your ability to communicate. Imagination is an integral aspect of all communication with Nature. Along with the whole-brain and pineal, it is the receptor and translator of Nature's flowing energy of natural communication. Without our human imagination we would be unable to communicate with Nature. Go with the flow . . . and TRUST.

A living question:

> *What is the best way to apply the teachings of nature in our lives?*
> *How can nature help us to integrate into our physical, materi-*
> *al-based living, apart from the obvious method of walking or*
> *being in nature? How can we apply the model nature exhibits into*
> *our life for measurable results?*

Hmm . . . I guess many people are already doing this. Permaculture and eco/organic farming are models of integrating with Nature, along with herbal medicines, etc., but I think I get your deeper point. Permaculture could be the model a person uses to feed their family, but does this change their inner relationship with themselves in a way that is less critical and more flowing? For me, a natural integration with Nature would require that people spend far more time in Nature as an observer. However, to take just a single aspect of this, we have unwittingly become onlookers of life, of our own lives, while Nature is a full-on participant. I have talked to people who, for years, have watched their lives spinning out of control . . . and they felt helpless. I pointed out that they were the onlooker, instead of the full participant in their life. This always surprised them, as they had never considered such a thing.

Nature is fully involved in the moment of life. Even the predators who spend much of their time sleeping, or observing the movements of their prey, are fully involved in the moment. *Nature lives consciously in the moment. Humanity lives subconsciously out of the moment.* If I was to take a single example from Nature for humanity to model itself from, it would be this: the ability to live consciously in the moment. And it is very possible, even though it is very challenging, and requires a level of commitment that very few people have. The big difference — with exceptions — is that the overall human expression is that of a single, finite, 'mortal' life. The overall expression of Nature is the endless continuity of life. Nature lives the bigger picture; humanity lives the smaller self-limited picture. Yes, we have religions that support the continuity of life through constant reincarnation, but even then most of these people, all the while maintaining this belief, live the smaller picture of want and desperation. Again — with exceptions. In humanity, there are always the exceptions. From my viewpoint, living the big picture in the moment would generate a quantum leap in human consciousness.

A curious question:

> *I'm curious as to what has to be aligned for Nature to connect with us and vice versa. I'm also wondering if Nature connects with the consciousness of individuals as well as groups. And how we support each other for a particular purpose, e.g., for the planet's benefit and/or for our own and others' growth. What is our symbiotic relationship with Nature and its purpose? I do feel/ know we are connected and have felt love and comfort through various experiences with birds and animals. Maybe this was a way of a manifestation in a form I would not be alarmed to re- ceive or experience.*

This whole book is about aligning our personal consciousness with the consciousness of Nature; being in the moment together. Regarding the group or individual connection, people vary. When, at an Intensive, I create an inner journey into Nature, I find that the group energy em- powers the experience for some people, yet for others they are more easily distracted by the occasional cough, or bodies moving, whatever. Personally, I prefer my own individual experience, yet I cannot deny that while guiding a group I have had some very powerful experiences. Nature is about conscious connection, whether it is a single individual or a group is irrelevant to Nature. An individual who is consciously connected is definitely more powerful than a group with a more scat- tered consciousness.

It is impossible for a conscious connection with Nature to benefit a single person without benefitting all people. Despite the appearance of the illusion, there is no such thing as a single, separate person. Single bodies, yes, but all humanity is One energy . . . and One with Nature. Each time a single person makes a meaningful conscious connection with Nature, it is to the benefit of the Whole.

Yes, we do have a symbiotic relationship with Nature, but as a collective we have lost our purpose in this. We *are* Nature. Many individuals do live in a way that fulfils this symbiotic purpose, but most do not. Nature is the *natural* growth of consciousness; humanity is — or is intended to be — the *creative* growth of consciousness. While these remain apart, the huge potential is lost. Combined, as One, the creative and the natural would beneficially and holistically impact the planet and all life upon it to a very great degree. Unfortunately, humanity lives in the conceptual and false division of humanity *and* Nature. While we live encased in this illusion, we lose the potential of our conscious unity with Nature.

A dreaming question:

I have many dreams of the ocean. It is always an ocean that is unbelievably clear and unbelievably full of marine life — whales and turtles and sharks and colourful, thriving coral. I have read about other people and their nature dreams; is there a connection or a way to develop the connection through dreaming?

Your dreaming of the ocean may well be connected to your current emotional life. This is a possibility, not a stated fact. The ocean is very full and very clear; this suggests that although much is happening on an emotional level for you right now, you will be able to deal with it to the extent your emotions will be clear and unclouded, yet rich and full. This is an ideal. However, it may be that you have a deep interest in the ocean and marine life. This would suggest that living near the ocean and possibly finding a way to live whereby you are able to train with an aqualung and do scuba diving, would be very fulfilling for you.

I suggest that you would also benefit from learning and practicing lucid dreaming. Carolyn did this for many years. Lucid dreaming is when you are able to consciously control the direction of the dream. You allow the content of the dream to unfold as it will, but you take it in the directions that you intuitively feel will be of benefit for you. If physically diving is a problem, you can alternatively dive into an ocean that

171

is just as real through the developed ability of lucid dreaming. Amazon would have books on this subject. Never dismiss lucid dreaming as just a dream. Equally, never dismiss clearly detailed and colourful dreams as just a dream. This is consciousness bringing something to the fore that has spent too long in the background of your life.

A sandy question:

> *I have a garden that really isn't a garden. It's a bare patch of sand at present. How can I connect with this land and let it tell me what it wants to be? At the moment, couch grass is growing, which is not a crop I'd like to cultivate.*

Do you see the conflict in this? You say the sandy patch is growing couch grass — this is its choice, and yet you wish to know what it wants to grow that suits your choice! Okay, the patch of sandy soil will grow or support whatever appropriate seeds are sown or whatever weeds are on it. How can it tell you what it would like to grow when what it would like to grow is a concept in your head? It is a patch of sandy soil . . . it is as it is.

The question is, what would you like to grow on the sandy soil? It is as simple as that. If you had a well-developed garden with many plants, and you had a new plant to add to the garden, then yes, it is a good idea to walk around the garden with the plant and let it tell you where it will thrive best. I have done this many times. Sometimes I put the plant where *I* want it to go, because the plants choice does not work for me!

However, you have this piece of land. Do you want ornamentals? Do you want flowers? Do you want vegetables? Are you prepared to water the sandy soil and plants regularly? Do you have a dog that likes this sandy soil?

All these questions are the *real* questions to answer. Personally, for me, if I had a patch of sandy soil, I would fill it with succulents and cacti. Remember, all cacti are succulents, but not all succulents are cacti! This would be rather colourful and different, requiring almost no water, and the least maintenance.

A stressful question:

Can you feel stress suffered by trees and other plants? I am sure that I can. During hot weather I feel the calmness in my gardens and lawn once it is all watered.

Yes, I do feel the stress of trees and plants if, and when, they are stressed. During a prolonged drought I feel the stress of our whole garden very strongly. My challenge is to not take on the stress personally. The more attached I become to a plant or the garden, the more I feel its stress. For me, every drought is a lesson in 'letting go'. Quite a lot of the trees of certain species in the bush (forest) around my garden have died during the droughts of the last couple of decades. I felt the withdrawal and end of every tree. And yet, it is not the end of a tree, for all trees experience continuity. For me, droughts are a constant reminder to not get caught up in the physical reality. Admire its beauty, enjoy its energy, but do not get emotionally attached.

Once, many years ago when I lived in Tasmania, I visited a forest that had been plundered by the loggers of the wood chip industry. It was a scene of devastation, the rape and ruin of a forest, a desecration of natural beauty. I sat on a tree stump as I looked around me, and I wept. As my rather shocked emotions slowly stabilised, and I wiped the tears from my eyes, very slowly emerging into my inner eye I saw that the whole forest was standing, every tree, every plant, all growing in pristine, metaphysical perfection.

This was a good lesson for me. On a metaphysical level, on that higher bandwidth, it was untouched by the heavy, uncaring hand of greed. I realised that although we can violate the physical reflection of Nature, we are unable to interfere with the greater reality of Nature in all its metaphysical glory. That metaphysical forest would remain, no matter what happened to the physical land, for as long as was needed by Nature to express the consciousness of that forest.

Summary: In your own time and space, let go of the intellectual questions that trouble you . . . and Trust! Trust opens the door to the experience of a greater reality. I am not suggesting that you become gullible and naive, but I am suggesting that these two qualities hold hands with innocence. And the innocence of your inner child is a *very* close to Nature.

Chapter Twenty-Three

FENG SHUI AND NATURE

You wake up in the morning and immediately begin thinking. Those thoughts are energy; energy that is radiating from you out into the cosmos. Although this is not a physical happening, physicality is affected. In terms of energy, which is also consciousness, Nature is within your metaphysical field of energy. Nature is never in conflict with life. Equally, Nature is never an expression of conflict, even though an erupting volcano or an earthquake make it seem otherwise. Even when we see what we perceive as conflict within Nature, this is a reflection of our own human conflict. In other words, what we see is not what IS, it is our human perception of what is . . . and that is very different.

How life changes with the tide of years. In the first half of the 20th century, when my father farmed his land in England, feng shui was not even a concept on the fringe of his awareness. As I grew up, developing my love affair with Nature, feng shui was as unknown to me as the dark side of the moon. Even during my search for Self, I had never heard of feng shui, and then . . . feng shui was suddenly with us. I remember how we first struggled with its pronunciation: in the Western World it is usually pronounced 'fung shway'. I also remember reading of how this ancient Chinese knowledge could make life and living so much easier.

Now, all these years later, I have read little about it, nor do I follow it as a way of life. Nevertheless, I do see that it has a lot to offer. Not as a trendy concept, nor as a smart, with-it way of approaching life, but in its very essence. And what is that essence? For me, it is balance. Bruce, a one-time student of feng shui and a good friend of mine, defined feng shui as: "Taking the built environment [architectural, people-created] and putting it in flow [harmony] with universal energy [chi]." For me, this was and is a clear and excellent definition. It also defines a balanced way of life.

Most of us will never be architects, designing and actually placing the buildings on the land, but just about all of us will live in those buildings, work in them and, for better or worse, develop a relationship with them.

For me, the main physical expression of feng shui is the placement of such a building — your house for instance. How many architects have a truly aware, or even a basic, relationship with the Earth? Housing estates today are generally built on available land, although single, expensive homes may be on prime real estate. But this land is not just land. This land is part of the living body of our planet Earth and, as with all land, it has a resonating energy. How many of our architects or builders tune into that energy and upon intuitively reading it, act accordingly? The immediate environment is noted, yes, but not the actual energy of the land. How strange it is that we humans, with all our potential intelligence, do not use it to attune with, or bother to learn about, the energy resonance of the place where we plan to live. Energetically, where we live will obviously assert a very powerful influence on our lives.

Not all land is amenable to human living. The whole of planet Earth is a vast network of lines of energy, or ley lines. These are generally known as the meridians of the Earth. We have them in our own bodies. Animals are in perfect accord and harmony with this energy — they express natural feng shui! We humans, however, have such a narrow focus we seem to completely miss connecting with the energy of the land. Let me put it this way: if you build or buy a house on land where cows *will not lie down*, then you are unlikely to experience harmony in that house. The land will exert a negative influence on everyone in the house. Not a wrong or bad negative, but in the sense that it is not a polarisation that is favourable for harmonious human habitation. We are told that by practising good feng shui this energy field can be changed. I do not disagree, but I can assure you that there are many variables involved.

Let me explain the cow aspect of this. When I farmed in Tasmania, I noticed in most of my paddocks that there were certain areas where cows would *never* lie down to rest. Rather, they would congregate in various other areas to lie down, indicating that this was their definite choice. In twelve years on that farm, the cows never lay down in certain areas of the paddocks. To test this, I often lay in their shunned areas, and I always had a feeling of not-at-ease. Not bad or wrong negative, but the energy would not allow me to feel inner-relaxed! When I lay in their chosen areas, I felt inner-relaxed and very much at ease. Imagine this in a house where the cows would not lie down. Unlike us, they are far more sensitive to the energies of the Earth.

For me, feng shui truly begins when you wake up in the morning. The direction of your thoughts and feelings this new day are creating an energy flow which you — all unaware of — will follow. Thoughts that are in harmony with the Whole are going to offer a far better day than thoughts that are separative and negative. If you wake up with an awareness of feng shui, and decide to play with balance and harmony this new day, deliberately weaving such energy into the strands of your thinking, your speaking, your actions, your focus, you are going to have a very good day. Sadly, many people do almost the exact opposite with blame, anger and criticism. They then consider themselves unlucky as they continually destroy the potential of their day.

As a generalisation, human thinking is negative. It takes an effort not to be sucked into the daily maelstrom of human thought. The many forms of media are constantly bombarding you with a mostly negative and judgemental outlook on life, yet if you resist it with anger or criticism, you become part of, connected to, it. So you do not judge or resist; you ignore, or decline to be involved in the human loop of negativity. This is *living* feng shui. This will have far more effect on your life than where you stand the bird bath in your garden. While you are in the city, the bird bath placement offers little. And if you live the true feng shui of Self, the bird bath will matter even less, wherever you are.

Let us revisit the unfortunate house located where cows will not lie down. Seriously, this is a real handicap. If you are aware that your family is a reasonable one, not overly prone to negative thinking, or blame, yet you all struggle to be on good terms in the house, then moving location offers a good option. Tune in to your house. Meditate on the energy of your home. Home is house *and* land. What do you *feel* when you meditate on its energy? If there is a feeling of discord, a thread of *something wrong*, a subtle uncomfortable feeling, then be aware that this is the energy in which you are living.

Certainly it is possible for some feng shui consultants to help rebalance the energy, but only for some people. It is not quite as simple as, "Do this and this, take that away and put this there," and all will be well. For one family, or one person in the family, or some people, it may work very well, for others it may have little to no affect. Why? Because life is not a flow of energy *outside* of Self. Life is a flow of energy *within* Self, and Self is the nucleus of feng shui. It is about harmony within. The outside is not truly real, it is an illusion, and no matter how you play with them, illusions remain illusions.

You may well ask, "What about feng shui and Nature?" Let me put it this way. You wake up in the morning and immediately begin thinking. Those thoughts are energy — energy that is radiating from you out into the cosmos. Although this is not a physical happening, physicality is affected. In terms of energy, which is also consciousness, Nature is within your metaphysical field of energy. Nature is never in conflict with life. Equally, Nature is never an expression of conflict, even though an erupting volcano or an earthquake make it seem otherwise. Even when we see what we perceive as conflict within Nature, this is a reflection of our own human conflict. In other words, what we see is not what IS; it is our human perception of what is . . . and that is very different!

Nature is an expression of the harmony and flow of natural life. True feng shui is each one of us being both a part and the Whole of that natural expression; unfortunately, we have become strangers to natural. Animals are not involved in self-conflict, most humans are. Conflict creates a blockage or resistance in the available flow of energy within you. This energy flow is life. Nature never resists life and is unable to mentally go into conflict with itself, but people do these things all the time. Hence dis-ease.

I am only touching on the outer edges of the vast depths of true feng shui. As I said, feng shui is not my subject. But as soon as I explain one aspect, this in turn leads to another, which reveals another, and suddenly I see far beyond my knowledge. I see and experience life in holistic terms — nothing is separate — so I have to make a choice of where to end an explanation. This can be difficult when knowing that it is still only a part of the greater picture. Equally, I have to live my life on these terms.

Let me offer an example. In 2003, while my late wife and I were travelling on our annual tour of seminars and public talks around the world, increasingly my suitcase was being lost, or delayed, or mutilated. Not her two suitcases, but my single suitcase. She told me in no un-certain terms that this was my responsibility. Obviously, the normal human reaction is to blame the airlines. I mean, how could it be my fault? But I knew that in truth, we create the energy flow of our lives, and this includes . . . everything! As I reflected on the suitcase problem, I knew that in truth, it was a Michael Roads problem. My feng shui was way out of kilter! While I love giving the seminars and talks, I did not like travelling and I detested airports. I had been in too many, too frequently. At least, that was my excuse! My energy toward airports was in direct conflict with flow and harmony. Hence, my suitcase — a repre-sentation of my travelling — got delayed and/or damaged. I realised all this as we ended our 2003 South African, European and American tour, so I decided it was time to drastically change my attitude/energy on our upcoming Japanese tour.

Seriously, when, a couple of months later we left for Japan, I smiled my way into the airports, inner-sang as we travelled, enjoyed as always the talks and seminars, and smiled my way home, all in perfect harmony with my well-behaved suitcase. Definitely a much better way of travelling!

This is what feng shui is really about. Let me offer one more example.

In 1998, we added a large extension onto our house. A bulldozer came and gouged into the soil near the back door, taking the top five meters off a small hillock at the end of the house. As I watched, I became aware of a feeling of energy distress, but I dismissed it as my own emotions. As a keen and passionate gardener, I had an uncomfortable feeling that I was violating the Earth for our house extension.

When I went outside the next morning, concerned with my feeling, and planning to sit and meditate of the site, a clear and beautiful rainbow was arced over the site of the extension, so I assumed that all was well. The new extension was built, and we moved in. Wonderful!

About five months later, my late, sharp-eyed wife noticed termite activity in some wood of the new section, so I called the builder to come and check it out. To keep this brief, we were quite shocked at the volume of termites that had entered the house, where they had done a considerable amount of damage. It cost several thousand dollars to repair and replace. I took full responsibility for this, and we paid. I rejected the 'sue the builder to get the insurance' avenue. If I had followed through with my meditation on the site, all would have been energetically harmonised. But I misread — or ignored — the signs.

When I went out the morning after the hilltop was bulldozed, and I saw the rainbow, I assumed all was well. In hindsight, I learned that the extension certainly received the blessings of the Spirit of our Home, but it was my responsibility to create and maintain a flow of harmony on that bulldozed site. I inadvertently failed to do this. If I had attuned with that site, I would have felt the areas of discord and I could have easily harmonised them with my own focused field of energy.

Only about five species from the large family of termites are attracted to eat the wood in the houses of Oz. Those termites ignored the older timber-filled section of our house, focusing only on the new section over the disturbed soil. We created a serious Earth disturbance which I completely overlooked. Today, that area of land and house are in harmony with the Earth and Nature.

Since my experience with the termites, I have learned that it is not only the timber of our houses that attract them. It has been my observation that termites are attracted by human discord; by highly-strung emotions; and by strong negativity. This can be human negativity, even earth-based energy lines of discord, or both. I am convinced that human negativity, especially fear, is a strong attractant for termites.

Feng shui is about creating and living within a field of energy that is in harmony with the universe. You can learn to play with this energy, creating the flow of life that most honours you. Life has never been against you; only you can go against life. When you are consciously aware, focused, and balanced, you 'are' the harmony of the universe expressing in Self. In this state of consciousness, you become feng shui in action.

Summary: If feng shui is a technique that you practice, I have serious doubts about its potential. I am quite convinced that the ancient Chinese mystics who first created the way of feng shui held the energy of harmony in their own state of consciousness. When I am in harmony with myself, I am in harmony with my environment. This is the living essence of feng shui in Nature.

Feng shui can teach you that as you find the internal balance and harmony which accompanies life flowing within you, so you are perfectly primed to enter the secret world of Nature.

Chapter Twenty-Four

EXPANDING THE KEYHOLE!

Intellectually, most adults relate only to a physical Nature, ac-
cepting, as does everyone else, that this is all there is. But there
is so much more! How can we intellectually understand Nature,
when it is not an intellectual expression? It makes no sense! Like
us, Nature is an expression of conscious intelligence, but this, our
greatest potential, is abandoned, littering the classroom floors
where it was destroyed by the scissors of unintentional ignorance
and thoughtless separation.

As a public speaker, I have learned that repeating words from very different angles, or from a different perspective, can often allow a person to grasp the meaning that was eluding them. So also it is with the written word. In this chapter there may be a slightly repetitive factor, but I hope it comes from a very different perspective, offering you illumination into the subject.

Apart from a few exceptional people, our normal human relationship with Nature is rather like looking at the natural world through the proverbial keyhole. We see only the physical aspect of an energetically immense, conscious expression that far transcends the physical. We see and therefore experience an incredibly limited version of what Nature has on display.

To a child, all Nature is new. Given the chance, a child interfaces with a Nature that has no names, no labels. Grass is not green; it is not a lawn; it is Mystery. This is what a child connects with; Mystery. But the child grows, learning to walk and talk, then to read as their schooling begins. Names and labels are now being attached to Nature. That 'stuff' that tasted strange is now green grass, and Mystery is banished, along with that precious connection.

As we are taught more and more about Nature, so, without our ever realising it, we actually *know* less and less. Our intellectual knowledge grows, but our *direct knowing* recedes. Moving through our school grades, we are now pushed into an intellectual world that seeks to understand Nature, yet adding ever more of the labels of limitation. If once, as a child, we had a real connection with Nature, by the time we are an adult, the average student is locked out of any true relationship with a metaphysical Nature.

Intellectually, most adults relate only to a physical Nature, accepting, as does everyone else, that this is all there is. But there is so much more! How can we intellectually understand Nature, when it is not an intellectual expression? It makes no sense! Like us, Nature is an expression of conscious intelligence, but this, our greatest potential, is abandoned, littering the classrooms floors where it was destroyed by the scissors of unintentional ignorance and thoughtless separation.

Throw away the keyhole — if you can — and let me give you a different, considerably larger view. The Nature that we see and relate to on Earth is the physical reflection of a vast, holistic, intricate, metaphysical and universal Nature. In *everything* in life, the metaphysical precedes the physical. There are no exceptions. Consider the implications of this!

When all this becomes your inner knowing — not a concept — your actual reality, then your whole relationship with Nature and life is forever changed. You are now able to have a relationship with the non-physical Nature that cannot be physically seen or touched, but which can be experienced and listened to. Nature communicates, but nobody is listening. We have lost the skill. We no longer realise that there is a vast difference between hearing and listening. Two people talk to each other, but neither truly listens; they hear. We can hear and think, but we cannot listen and think. Thinking takes us out of the moment . . .

we cannot think our way into the moment. To listen, we are required to be in the moment. This means that to listen to the inaudible voice of Nature, we have to be in the moment. We are not good at this! It means being fully conscious.

Although you have read similar words earlier, the above words are a mere flicker of insight concerning the vast, metaphysical connection with Nature that is possible. In this chapter I am responding to a request for my comment on the *emanations* that are apparent in their photographs of tree trunks and rock faces.

It is an interesting, and very ambiguous subject. I have noticed on our eroded mountains in Australia that when a human face is apparent in a cliff face, it is always an Aboriginal face. When I have seen such human faces in North America in the rock structure of mountains, they are always native American Indian. I am told on good authority that it is the same in New Zealand, where it is a Maori face that is apparent. I find this fascinating, because the Aboriginals of Australia where not the first people on this land, nor were the Maori the first people of New Zealand. I think maybe the same is true of North America. If we go back a few hundred thousand years in Oz, when the land-plate was in a very different geographical location, there were people of another race here. They have left their evidence in rock paintings that pre-date Aboriginal rock art — but I have yet to see one of their faces apparent in the cliffs or rock structures of Australia. Why are they not in the rocks, or have their images completely eroded away?

I have learned that to metaphysically journey into a metaphysical Nature/reality, we have to leave behind our intellect that seeks to understand, utilising instead our conscious intelligence. This opens us to the experience of mystical cognition. The inner knowing that emerges from mystical cognition is always holistic, far transcending a linear, intellectual understanding. Our attempts to intellectually understand Nature is the same as looking through the proverbial keyhole and then conceptualising what it is we cannot see. Far better to open the door which contains the keyhole, and walk through the doorway into a greater metaphysical reality: the boundless, multi-dimensional, metaphysical reality to which we are soul born.

Attempting to explain, understand, and intellectually chase the mystical emanations that you may photograph and/or film will slowly but gradually push you back to — and through — the keyhole. If, however, you are able to embrace the Mystery of the emanations, not needing explanation and understanding, then the spirits of Nature that they represent will be able to take you on a conscious journey into that greater reality. In this way we become open to the potential of drawing back the veil of separation between self and Nature.

I liken this to being again a child, even whilst we are an adult. Is it so difficult to still the mind in a forest, and imagine the wonder and awe that a three year old child might feel. To really connect with the inner child, but to walk on legs that are strong and true. A forest is not just a lot of trees. I remember so well as a child of all I did not know. I was in awe of Byron's Pool Woods in Grantchester, Cambridgeshire. It was a place of wonder for me, a place of intrigue and Mystery. When, as an adult, I have attempted to retraced my childhood steps, I was unable to bring back that very different experience of my child-self in the woods. Since then, I have walked rainforests in Oz and I have been able to re-kindle that childlike awe and wonder to a rather limited degree. We pay a toll for growing up!

Summary: In whatever way is meaningful to you, do your best to expand the keyhole through which you view life. If you deny that you see life through a keyhole, then know that the key is now blocking it. This is a shame. It takes a fair measure of humility to accept that the limitations of cleverness do exist, and it takes even more humility to accept your inherent greatness.

Chapter Twenty-Five

THE GARDENS OF LIFE

This is where the relationship truly come to the fore. Loving the garden, loving the land, loving the plants; really loving Nature — this creates a conscious relationship with Nature. In this great relationship, the garden is your meeting place with Nature. You are the student and Nature is the teacher. But something extra is required. Nature lives in the eternal moment. Plants are not thinking about us, or their place in the world; they are simply growing and living in the moment

There are many gardeners in the world, but few are outstanding. What is it that makes one particular gardener stand out from so many others? First and foremost, it is the relationship that the gardener has with their garden. And it *is* a relationship! Some gardeners enjoy looking after the garden, and they have a marvellous garden, while for many others — who do not actually qualify as gardeners — it is the bane of the their life: mowing the lawn, hedge-trimming, pulling weeds — *ugh*, pruning roses — ouch. The garden has become an exhausting battlefield. Enough!

Let us be clear; you can be a very good gardener by following the books and doing as they suggest. Repetition can make a person into a good gardener; learning the ropes, so to speak. It is not at all difficult to be a good gardener — but *outstanding*? That takes something extra; something beyond technique, something beyond knowledge, something beyond following a subconscious programme of gardening success.

This is where the relationship truly comes to the fore. Loving the garden, loving the land, loving the plants; really loving Nature — this creates a conscious relationship with Nature. In this great relationship, the garden is your meeting place with Nature. You are the student and Nature is the teacher. But something extra is required. Nature lives in the eternal moment. Plants are not thinking about us, or their place in the world; they are simply growing and living in the moment.

Unfortunately, we think our way out of the moment, we cannot think our way into it. This means, in effect, that while all natural life is living consciously in the moment, humanity is so busy thinking that we are compelled to live subconsciously. We are rarely consciously conscious of actually *living* in the moment. In this way our subconscious living and Nature's conscious living are unable to mesh and merge. You cannot be a subconscious gardener, and Love the garden, because Love is a conscious expression. Very much enjoy the garden, yes, without a doubt.

As a gardener, you may quarrel or argue with your spouse, but never with the garden. For this type of person, the garden is a often a retreat, a refuge, a shelter from the stormy blasts! Sorry, but this does not create an *outstanding* gardener! You may be a gardener who wants and achieves the most flower-filled garden in the street. Very nice, a good gardener; sorry, but still not outstanding. You cannot be an outstanding gardener and use the garden as an outlet for your frustrations, or ambitions. Wrong energy. When you go into a garden thinking of problems, or worrying, or angry, or any other negative distractions, your energy-field changes; you lower the intensity and quality of your Light-energy. This, in turn, has a negating effect on the energy-field of the garden; once again, no chance of being an outstanding gardener.

Let us leave all the regular gardening people and focus on the qualities of an outstanding gardener. For them, their garden is life.

In my book, *Conscious Gardening,* I describe an outstanding gardener as a person who is fully involved with the garden all the time they are in it. Why is this so important? A garden is a large field-of-energy;

187

you, also, are a field-of-energy. If this energy could be physically seen, it would appear as Light. If you look on your physical garden and your life as one and the same garden, then you will be an outstanding gardener of life.

When I was around ten or twelve years of age in England, I met a lady in her nineties. She was the great aunt of a school friend. Knowing that I had a large collection of plants, she invited me to see her garden. It was one small garden in the middle of a row of terraced houses, each garden divided from the others by a three metre (ten feet) high brick wall. The sunlight struggled to find her garden, but for most of the year it was filled with an abundance of flowering plants. I was already a keen gardener, and I knew there was not enough sun to bring those plants into flower. Sun is the flowering factor for most — not all — plants. This whole situation puzzled me.

As I watched her, feeling the Love she had for her garden, I had a great insight. I realised that *she was the sun* in her garden. I learned that when you Love the garden and its plants as she did, you can throw the rule book away. She provided the sun energy that her plants needed. Without a doubt, she was the first outstanding gardener I ever met. I never forgot her — or what she taught me about the power of human Love without ever even mentioning it!

One of the great lessons I have consciously learned from Nature in a garden, is about *being-with* while *doing-to*. We get so busy, doing, doing, doing — all the while thinking about our day. Doing-to, but not being-with! If you are pulling weeds, be aware of what you are doing — be with it. In this way you will gradually become conscious of a greater connection with Nature. Nature speaks, but nobody is listening. We think hearing is listening; it is not. Listening takes place in the moment — but nobody's home! Conscious gardening means that you are learning to be conscious in life, and your teacher is Nature. The garden is the meeting place, you are the student. Nature offers you the most wondrous possibilities, taking you beyond the mundane and into the magnificent. All this, by developing a deep and creative relationship and connection between the garden and life.

Some people talk of the spirit of Nature; this is found as a higher energy in the gardens of the true garden lovers. These are the 'green thumb' people. Their gardens may be huge and beautiful, or a sprawl of seemingly untidy plants, but energy-wise they have the X-factor. Equally, a garden may be tiny, as with the elderly lady I mentioned previously, but the relationship with the garden can be huge. When you can follow the intuitive 'feelings' you have as a conscious gardener, placing plants in the ground where *they* prefer to grow, you will be able to develop that precious Nature/human relationship to its full potential.

This is when you become aware of the clear parallels between life and the garden. Pruning old, sprawling, thorny growth from the roses, equates to removing the tangle of prickly attitudes we develop, hindering our growth. If we are conscious while we clear away unwanted weeds from the garden, allowing our plants the room to grow, we can also release the weeds of our old critical, often aggressive habits, giving space for the expansion and growth of our own potential.

You will realise at this point of the book that connecting *with* Nature is far more than it first appears to be. It is a skill, a natural art, an inner potential inherent in all humanity. This begs the question; if it is natural to us, why is it so rarely apparent? To connect with Nature you are required to use your whole-brain and heart connection. Most people seldom do this. Most people use a left-brain connection only. This means that most people attempt to have an intellectual relationship with Nature or life, which is not possible. We have lost our fundamental connection with Nature. We are no longer *truly* living life, and sadly, we are no longer consciously aware of our own spiritual truth . . . the soul Beings we are.

You need to be really clear about what I have written so far. If you would like to truly participate in Nature *and in your own life,* rather than remain as an onlooker, you cannot bypass the reality of consciously re-connecting with your own greater truth — the immortal Being you truly are. Entering the secret world of Nature is not about your mortal personal self, it is about your immortal universal self.

I have had a deep relationship with Nature for most of my life. Currently, my life is a process of moving ever deeper into the metaphysical realms of Nature and life . . . and sharing this in my books. You need to well and truly grasp and accept that the Nature you see and relate to is no more than the physical reflection of a vast metaphysical Nature. Like *Alice in Wonderland*, we need to go through that mirror reflection . . . into a greater reality. Obviously, we cannot do this physically, so we need to use our metaphysical Light-body to go into the greater metaphysical reality.

As I have written, you will need patience. You will also need to learn the art of listening. A cat listens, we just hear. Listening comes from the moment, and is a conscious act. Hearing is happening while we may be otherwise involved; this is subconscious and mostly involuntary. Listening invokes a deeper, quieter, part of us; it is the whole-brain, heart-soul connection.

We all have constant thoughts; this is the mind endlessly regurgitating its mental nonsense. No thoughts, and there is Silence . . . and in this Silence there is a song of power. Not your power, or Nature's power, just power. But, you can connect with, and use this power, so long as you do not personalise it. To do this requires trust. You must trust yourself. Not easy! To connect *with* Nature means that this power is the conduit between your trust, you, and Nature. All are necessary. Once this conduit is activated, Nature and self are revealed as One. I repeat . . . we *are* Nature.

When you connect with Nature you are able to communicate with it. It takes a big leap in consciousness to listen to a tree communicate with you, and *know* that this is not a fabrication of the mind. I have read several other peoples Nature communications, and have *known* them to be false. And this is okay; neither right nor wrong. Equally, I have read quite a few others, and *known* them to be true communication. Soul knows. If you think this sounds arrogant . . . so be it! I, certainly, had my time of not knowing the difference between the subtle mind and the subtlety of inner-communication. With a lot of practice and plenty of self-trust, you eventually arrive at a good place. Criticising and berating yourself for your lack of patience, constant inattention, your assumed inability, or your lack of self-trust, or focus — or, all of these put to-gether — gets you nowhere.

When you sit down, become silent, and consciously focus on a tree, you and tree energetically connect. You share One field of energy. Tree is not outside Self. This is where communicating with Nature truly begins. While you perceive the tree and yourself as separate — *you* talk *with* tree — you are playing mind games. And believe me, mind has an endless repertoire. Trees do not think or talk, but trees are a living repository of an immense amount of conscious experience. This is not necessarily all tree experience; this is quite often Earth/life experience. As I have already previously stated, trees are an expression of conscious intelligence, but they have no intellect. Trees are completely impersonal; but trees are always consciously connected with us. Our being discon-nected from them does not mean that they are disconnected from us. It is we who have to reawaken the connection, not them. Trees experience Oneness, separation does not exist in Nature/life. They communicate with us in their conscious expression of growth, but nobody is taking any notice. We are busy, busy, busy.

To re-connect *with* Nature, all this has to change within us. You cannot connect *with* Nature and remain the person you currently are. You have to expand in consciousness and grow. This is the thrust and the clear message implicit in the pages of this book. You are a pow-erful Being, every person is, but most are in denial of their power. To enter the secret world of Nature requires you to take back your inherent power.

Many people get confused over the differences between power and force. (I recommend the book *Force Versus Power* by Dr. David Hawkins.) We have a military force, a police force, and the enforcement of our laws. All this is imposed upon us. Force is generally an outside influence on us, while your power comes from within. You cannot force your way into the secret world of Nature, but with your own inner self-empowerment, it will open to you.

Gentleness is power; humility is power. Self-trust is a huge power, far beyond anything that I can explain in these pages. In the briefest possible explanation, self-trust literally reshapes your world. And that is powerful!

If, having read all this, you decide you want to learn to consciously communicate with Nature . . . you will be pushed to grow, to expand, to become more flexible; the very process will demand it. You will discover that once you get out of the box that most people live in — and re-connect — there is a huge and wondrous greater reality waiting to welcome you.

And long has it waited.

AFTERWORD

You will quickly realise that this is a repeat of some of the second chapter, the structure of reality. Why am I repeating it here? If you read this on the first pass through this book, I am sure that you would have registered its value. I lament that I knew nothing of such things when I struggled and limped my way into Nature's secret world, it would have been so much easier. Yet all this came in perfect timing for this particular book; not before. To me, this is significant. For that reason I am presenting its essence once again for your perusal. To comprehend fully the meaning of the bandwidths will surely be the key to your success.

Okay . . . imagine a centrifuge into which is thrown many full shovels of various sized rocks, stones, gravel, various types of sand and soil, along with some water and ice. A concrete mixer is a good physical example, but imagine it spinning at a very great speed. As the centrifuge spins, all the rocks, stones and gravel and sand/soil particles, water and ice are thrown outward to their varying positions as determined by their weight and density. Now take away all outer limits to the centrifuge — let go of the cement mixer — increase to infinity the amount thrown into the centrifuge and everything in it will be compelled ever outward to reach its own outer limits in space. And this will vary greatly.

In your imagination, expand this centrifuge out until it is the size of our universe and spinning at the speed of light. Okay . . . now imagine a series of bandwidths from the outer limits to the inner centre of this immense universal centrifuge. There are literally thousands of these bandwidths from the outer limits of density to the very centre of Light. Just as with a radio we need to know the bandwidth to be able to tune into a certain station, so these cosmic bandwidths indicate the reality of structure and the structure of reality via the density of their frequency. Obviously, all similar densities end up in the same bandwidth. These bandwidths are often referred to as parallel universes, for they all occupy the same apparent space, while appearing to be parallel to us.

You will probably not be surprised to learn that our 3-dimensional physical density bandwidth is close to, but not fully at, the outer limits of this vast, universal centrifuge. Now, however, the explanation becomes a bit more complex. In Truth we are metaphysical souls and, as such, our energy is very light, not at all dense, yet we live our 3-dimensional lives in physical bodies. Unfortunately we have taken on the limits of this physical density even though it does not represent the truth of who we are. To make matters even worse, we do not live our lives as a light-soul in the dense-physical, we live our lives as a dense-physical in our physical density.

As we look at, and experience the world around us in and from our dense physical reality, we are unable to see the structure of reality on other bandwidths for they are beyond our frequency spectrum of sight and sound — even though they occupy the same space! Over aeons of time we have taken on the belief that we are physical Beings, living within our limits as though we are living life fully. As becomes obvious, we are only living a fraction of the potential of our true, metaphysical soul reality. To make the situation even more clear, we are physically 3-dimensional while all the expressions of our mental, intuitive, and emotional bodies are 4-dimensional . . . and yet we continue our lives within the confines and restrictions of living our limits!

Let me present it another way. These are a few of our bodies:

A *Mental* body and an *Emotional* body.	——	Both these bodies are invisible on our physical spectrum. Both are metaphysical.
Etheric body.	——	This is the energy interface between the physical and the metaphysical bodies. All these bodies combine to make up our astral body.
Astral body.	——	As souls, we are astral Beings. In other words, we are immortal metaphysical Beings who are living our lives immersed and lost in mortal physical bodies.
Our Physical body	——	The physical body is within a more dense bandwidth than our metaphysical bodies, yet it occupies exactly the same space as our mental, emotional, etheric and astral bodies.

When I travel metaphysically, I move my focus of Self away from the physical body into my Light-body. Light-body is my name for the mental, emotional and etheric bodies that make up the astral body. However, I am awake and conscious when I do this, not asleep. The astral body of everyone moves away from the physical body in deep, rapid eye movement (REM) sleep. If this were to suddenly not happen there would quickly be mass insanity.

Okay, let us now return to the bandwidths. Just as the outer band-width is 1st and 2nd dimensional, the next is our familiar 3rd and 4th dimensions, then the 5th and 6th dimensions and so on — although we quickly reach a point where dimensions cease to have any meaning to us. Every bandwidth has its own frequency: the higher the frequency the greater is the expression of the reality of structure and the more complex the structure of reality to experience life. It gets even more fascinating when you realise that every bandwidth occupies the same place in space. Actually, it occupies the moment, rather than space, but we so seldom experience the fullness of life in the moment that we have become addicted to linear time and space.

At this point you may be thinking; "What's he talking about with our third and fourth dimension?" So let me explain once again. We are physically 3-dimensional, but metaphysically, we are 4-dimensional. All our thoughts, our emotions, feelings, intuition, imagination, etc. are obviously not physical; they are metaphysical and express on a 4th dimensional reality. It should again be noted and remembered that the metaphysical always precedes the physical.

The view of our solar system from our 3rd- 4th-dimensional viewpoint is totally different from the view in a 5th- 6th-dimensional reality . . . and so on. We experience so-called space and distance and connect it with linear time: we then call this eternity. Like you, I see this physically, but when I move into a 5th-dimensional reality in my Light-body, I see it very differently: there is no space and distance, and all time occupies the same moment. This is when you are able to experience and comprehend the greater reality of what we call God. A God that we have rendered in our own image and reduced to fit in our very limited 3rd- 4th-dimensional conceptual understanding.

Starting from close to the outer, most dense bandwidth, and moving inward our comprehension of the universe increases exponentially; that is if we like to metaphysically undertake the journey. And comprehension is rather different from understanding. Understanding is based in the intellect, while comprehension is based in our intelligence. I comprehend much that I do not understand, nor do I need to. We have turned understanding into a hurdle, for it represents the dense level frequency of structure attempting to understand a higher frequency level of structure, and this is not possible. However, if you move your higher metaphysical frequency into the higher frequency of the structure you are attempting to understand, you will then experience and quite easily comprehend the greater reality of it. Simple, huh?

In our metaphysical body we have seven basic chakras affecting the physical body and five chakras affecting the metaphysical body. A chakra is a spinning wheel of light/colour energy. Even if you are familiar with this, maybe I can give you further insight into what this means: The first seven chakras connect you with the physical world, with Nature, with the elements and the elementals.

Red base chakra connects you with earth.
Orange sacral chakra connects you with water.
Yellow solar plexus chakra connects you with fire.
Green heart chakra connects you with air.
Blue throat chakra connects you with the etheric.
Indigo brow chakra connects you with universal wisdom.
Violet crown chakra connects you with a greater reality.

The next five chakras all connect the metaphysical you with the essence of a much higher frequency spectrum/bandwidth:

The ultra-violet eighth chakra connects you *with your higher spiritual potential, offering illumination and higher communication.*

The rainbow colours of your ninth chakra connects you *with the blueprint of the soul you are through your many incarnations/ lives.*

The pure light energy of your tenth chakra connects you *with your divine creativity and the synchronicity of life.*

The brilliant rose light of your eleventh chakra connects you *with Self in other dimensions and realities of the higher spectrum.*

The intense blazing miniature sun of your twelfth chakra connects you *with the vast metaphysical universe to which you can now listen, and experience.*

I need to add that none of these chakras open automatically. As you grow in consciousness, so the chakras develop and open. The higher chakras need to be consciously opened to be experienced. This is a natural process of conscious evolution in the growth of a human Being.

Caution: Never, I repeat, never get involved with people who claim to open chakras. This is seriously unnatural and metaphysically damaging. A very dangerous, and often disastrous, practice.

At my 5-Day Intensives I teach people how they can develop and open their chakras. This promotes conscious spiritual growth which in turn raises a person's frequency, opening them to, and connecting them with higher, finer bandwidths.

All these bandwidths of universal life suggests that, whether we live it or not, we have the capacity and potential of living as multidimensional Beings. What a paradox; the incredible diversity beyond our sight and sound is as close to us as our breath, yet as far away from our experience as the furthest star and our unshakeable belief in separation.

Finally, maybe now you will have a better comprehension of Pan. Pan means 'all.' Pan occupies every bandwidth simultaneously. Pan is an ancient, vast conscious Intelligence that occupies all the frequencies of the infinite spectrum. Even I, for the first time, have a better comprehension of the very magnitude of Pan. It is very humbling, but never reducing.

I have done my best in these pages to introduce you to the secret metaphysical world of Nature. We all easily see the physical bandwidth of Nature and thus we are inclined to believe that Nature is purely physical, just as we believe ourselves to be, but it is not so. The bandwidth of a higher frequency metaphysical Nature is sharing the same space/moment as all physical form. This higher frequency is where our *deeper* connection with Nature takes place. It is to this higher frequency that this book is designed to guide you. Hold hands with Trust . . . *and fly.*

I could wish you good luck, but good luck is the meeting place of preparation and opportunity. If you inner-grow in the ways that I have outlined, you will be prepared. Once you are prepared, then in your own perfect timing, the opportunities will continually arise.

ABOUT MICHAEL J. ROADS

Michael Roads was born a farmer's son in Cambridgeshire, England, in 1937. From an early age he discovered that he had a natural ability to travel beyond linear time and space, and enter into deep communication with Nature. Since his spiritual enlightenment at age 49, Michael has written 21 books on his experiences and many explorations of alternate realities and dimensions. His main focus and teachings are based in *unconditional* Love and emotional balance.

The year 2018 marks his 27th year of traveling over five continents presenting inspirational and life-changing 5-Day Intensives in a clear, compelling, humorous and no-nonsense format, enabling many participants to experience profound shifts in consciousness.

Michael, a modern mystic, weaves his wealth of life experiences with the most extraordinary insights — insights that offer pathways to our deep spiritual relationship with Nature and with Self. He has both the consciousness and the ability to empower people to gain understanding of the true nature of reality, and assist them in their spiritual awakening to their Divine potential.

For the international tour schedule and additional information please visit:

www.michaelroads.com

RoadsLight Pty Ltd
P.O. Box 778
Nambour, QLD 4560
Australia
office@michaelroads.com

SIX DEGREES PUBLISHING GROUP
"Books that transcend the ordinary"

CPSIA information can be obtained
at www.ICGtesting.com
Printed in the USA
LVHW090154270421
685686LV00005B/48